Shadow Self

Shadow Self

How to
Finally Confront Our Failures
and Find New Life

Mark Chironna

invite
PRESS

Plano, Texas

Be like the fox
who makes more tracks than necessary,
some in the wrong direction.
Practice resurrection.
                    —Wendell Berry, "Manifesto:
            The Mad Farmer Liberation Front"

See the complete text at
https://bookpeopleblog.com/2011/04/05
/poem-of-the-day-manifesto-the-mad-farmer
-liberation-front/.

CONTENTS

PREFACE

Between the quiet solitude of our hearts and the noisy chaos of the world, we find ourselves dodging life's shadows—the seemingly unknowable or malignant vestiges of our unfinished business that refuse to be dispersed. We long instead for a glimmer of hope, a breath of life that whispers of renewal and rebirth. These pages are written as a heartfelt invitation for us to journey together from the depths of despair to the high peaks of transformation. More than mere pages and words, this book opens a shared pilgrimage toward understanding and embracing the resurrection life that is promised to each of us.

Life, in its unpredictable rhythm, brings black swan events that can change everything in the blink of an eye. Unexpected and profound, such moments challenge us to find a steadfast anchor in the storm. In the spirit of the apostle Paul, we learn to count all as loss compared to the surpassing greatness of knowing Christ and the power of his resurrection. Therefore, our journey is about rising, shedding the chains that hold us back, and stepping into the light of a new day.

The poetic eloquence of Wendell Berry, as shown in this book's epigraph, speaks of practicing resurrection—an act of defiant hope that chooses life over the entropy of despair.[1] What if, in this practice, we find the courage to be like the fox, leaving more tracks than necessary—some in the wrong direction—as a testament to our relentless pursuit of life? Jesus, the "Mad Farmer," liberates us to live this resurrection, embracing a prophetic madness that is, in truth, the sanest response to a world in turmoil.

The story of the tragic biblical hero, King Saul, reminds us that we are part of a larger narrative that has been unfolding since the dawn of time. By comparing and contrasting Saul's life with fictional lives from the cinematic pantheon of superheroes and elsewhere, we will see how our failures and triumphs ultimately offer lessons and legacies that enrich our paths. As we traverse the current landscapes of vulnerability, anxiety, fear, and division, we do so with the knowledge that we are not alone. Our stories are interwoven with those of countless others who have walked this earth, each seeking the same truth, the same light.

This book is for you—the weary traveler, the hopeful seeker, the broken yet unyielding spirit. Together, we will explore what it means to practice resurrection in every aspect of our lives. We'll delve into our vulnerabilities, confront our fears, mourn our losses, and, most importantly, celebrate our resilience and capacity for renewal.

As we stand on the threshold of a new day, let's commit to this journey with open hearts and willing spirits. Let's embrace the challenges and changes, knowing that each step forward leads us to become more fully human and alive. The path won't be easy, but the destination—a life imbued with the depth, beauty, and mystery of resurrection—is worth every hardship.

So come. Let's begin this exodus together, from the shadows into the magnificent dawn.

Dr. Mark Chironna

Notes

1. Wendell Berry, "Manifesto: The Mad Farmer Liberation Front," in *The Mad Farmer Poems* (Berkeley, CA: Counterpoint, 2014).

INTRODUCTION
Cultural Chaos and the Power of Myth

Every era has its heroes and villains. At times, society and culture enter intensely seismic seasons—periods of sheer chaos and ever-escalating uncertainty. In those times, our awareness of heroes and villains is sharpened, and our insistence on heroes declares our fears. Rummaging through the unsettledness, we seek solace in the pantheon of fictional and mythological characters and even historical figures who will give meaning to the madness and display the virtues we long to cultivate in ourselves.

Often, we take our heroes and villains where we find them. Just as often, they present themselves through comic books and the silver screen. My childhood was enlivened by the DC and Marvel comics I read and collected (and wish I still owned). I marveled at the adventures of Spider-Man, the Avengers, the Fantastic Four, Captain America, Superman, Batman, and so many others. They were mythic characters—invulnerable, almost god-like heroes who shaped my budding understanding of bravery and justice. As stalwarts of virtue, honor, and dignity, they made every tale seem clear-cut. And in their world of good versus evil, good always seemed to prevail.

In my middle years, I noticed a shift in the larger cultural narrative. The disenchantment and disillusionment of postmodernity proved that beloved comic narratives and superheroes were not immune to cultural tectonics. The stories that once offered escape and inspiration began to mirror the ambiguities of life in the real world. Bald-faced beacons of justice became more enigmatic as characters like Batman explored moral dilemmas and their dark sides as they grappled with outer and inner demons.

A tragic event seemed to typify the shift. The late Heath Ledger's hauntingly brilliant portrayal of the Joker in *The Dark Knight* was soon followed by the actor's untimely death.[1] His immersion into the Joker's anarchic and tormented psyche left an indelible mark on Heath's character and his audiences alike. His passing shocked us and released waves of reflection about the impact of delving too deeply into the darkness of iconic characters—a ritual now emblematic of our search for meaning.

The Cinematic Mirror

From ancient myths to our modern-day superheroes, the winning ways of larger-than-life characters have always captivated humanity. While they fuel our unspoken hopes and dreams, they also reflect our existential fears, anxieties, and profound questions about our existence and the future we face. The cinematic universe is both respite from our current reality and a mirror drawing us back into what we try to escape. Every superhero's story reflects our dreams, our darkest moments, and our hoped-for resurrections.

The DC and Marvel franchises have cornered their market and genre with the power of story and the mastery of metaphor. Over the years, their epics have documented our life experiences as individuals and as a culture, becoming a kind of mythical libretto through which we read about ourselves. The films' motifs parallel many of the themes of this book, demonstrating on a visual and narrative level what we as a culture are celebrating, suffering, and longing to comprehend.

From the perspective of personal growth and an acknowledgment of our human frailty, we will briefly explore a handful of films released in a four-year span. These iconic cinematic adventures register many of the moods and metaphors rumbling through our cultural lithosphere. These rumbles are not random but noteworthy as part of a shared experience that largely occurs on a deeply unconscious level. As you read, therefore, notice the recurring human themes the films present—not so much with the eye of a film critic but as an observer of what they evoke and invoke in relation to the human condition. Strange as it might seem, these cinematic reflections of real-life rumblings can speak to our exodus from the shadows.

Batman v Superman: Dawn of Justice (2016)[2]

The title of this film forecasts its departure from the simple heroics that marked similar films and comics during my youth. Its depiction of a conflict between revered superheroes is unprecedented. We see Batman (aka Bruce Wayne, a rich, tech-savvy multimillionaire who uses his resources to fight crime) and Superman (a superhuman from the planet Krypton whose powers are unparalleled) not as unblemished paragons of virtue but as deeply flawed beings driven by ego, fear, and misunderstanding. Their hostile interaction shocked fans who never expected their heroes to be at odds.

Excerpts from the film drive home the rift between the icons. During an altercation, Superman tells his temporarily downed opponent, "Stay down! If I wanted it, you'd be dead already!"[3] As the skirmish continues, Batman schools Superman, saying, "You're not brave. Men are brave. It's time you learned what it means to be a man."[4] In another heated exchange, Superman tells Batman, "Next time they shine your light in the sky, don't go to it. The Bat is dead. Bury it. Consider this mercy."[5] Batman replies, "Tell me. Do you bleed?" Without answering, Superman rockets upward as Batman adds, "You will."[6]

The once unthinkable conflict between these giants mirrors the fomenting unrest and disillusionment particularly evident from 2010 through 2015 as economic crises, political upheaval, social movements, and environmental concerns dominated headlines and the collective consciousness. Ever the mirror to society's soul, Hollywood responded with riveting narratives of unrest and complexity that resonated with our struggles and illuminated our existential and unconscious narratives.

Capturing the aura of cultural instability, *Superman v Batman* delivered a shocking twist in which Superman, the seemingly immortal icon, falls, leaving the world to mourn the loss of its greatest protector, its long-standing symbol of hope and justice. Lois Lane stands over his grave and sprinkles a handful of dirt onto the casket deep below. As the soil lands, a subtle but unmistakable rumble begins, promising that all is not lost. The story is far from over.

Justice League (2017)[7]

The narrative of this film makes it clear that no single hero can confront the world's challenges alone, so it proposes a union of heroes that gathers its strength from every corner of the DC universe. Despite the overwhelming assembly of power, Superman's absence looms large. In the mounting sense of existential threat, the fallen hero's presence seems irreplaceable.

Amid an atmosphere of grief, determination, and technological ingenuity, the story moves toward Superman's resurrection. His return, however, is not without complexity. Once an unquestioned emblem of virtue and self-control, Superman now grapples with his unresolved vulnerabilities and a repressed anger that blurs the line between vengeance and justice. Confronting his own inner tumult, the hero once asked by Batman whether he bleeds now lifts Batman off the ground with an almost choking grip and asks him, "Do you bleed?"[8]

This evolved, complex narrative reflects every human's journey, reminding us that resurrection and moments of triumph coexist with the struggle for balance, justice over revenge, and resolution over rage. The film is a testament to the enduring human spirit and the continuous call to rise, transform, and aspire to a higher calling.

Wonder Woman (2017)[9]

This twenty-first-century rendition of *Wonder Woman* points to a broader discourse on women's roles and challenges the status quo in imagery and dialogue. When Diana (Wonder Woman) explains her mission to her mother, Queen Hippolyta, the queen says, "You know that if you choose to leave, you may never return."[10] Rejecting fear and refusing to be passive, Diana replies, "Who will I be if I stay?" Likewise, when American Army Air Service pilot Steve Trevor warns Diana off her plan and says, "I can't let you do this," she owns her cause, draws a line, and tells him, "What I do is not up to you."[11]

Wonder Woman taps into the tension created by toxic patriarchal structures that continue to undermine the place of women. The narrative reminds us to honor the feminine archetype in both sacred and secular realms, advocate for a more equitable and respectful understanding of the feminine, and embrace a theology that genuinely reflects the dignity and equality of all human beings. The character of Diana emerges as a counternarrative to traditional, often repressive depictions of women. She embodies strength, wisdom, and compassion, and she invites us to reexamine the potential of women as leaders, warriors, and influential figures in shaping society.

The depiction is relevant despite the considerable strides toward gender equality over the past century and a half. The film speaks to pervasive biases that remain evident even in the entertainment industry that produces films like *Wonder Woman*. Similar biases persist in other corporate realms as well as religious communities.[12]

Black Panther (2018)[13]

Amid the persistence of racial injustice, this film resonates culturally and stands as a milestone, particularly in the context of American history. It presents not only a superhero narrative but a profound exploration of African heritage, identity, and the consequences of colonialism. Its vision of empowerment, unity, and progress challenges persistent racial stereotypes and systemic issues that have long plagued not only American society at large, but Hollywood itself.

Black Panther celebrates African culture, innovation, and resilience and depicts the Kingdom of Wakanda as a technologically advanced African nation untouched by colonialism. This powerful counternarrative to the timeworn image of Africa as a continent in need of saving reimagines what might have been had African nations not been subjected to colonialism and the slave trade.

The film doesn't shy away from Africa's complex issues, such as the legacy of oppression, the pain of the African diaspora, and the struggles Black people face regarding identity and belonging. *Black Panther* navigates the nuances of these realities, illustrating the internal and external conflicts that arise from a history caught between injustice and the quest for a better future.

The film also resonates with the reality that the progress made in civil rights has not rid the United States of systemic racism, inequality, and a reluctance to fully confront and rectify its past. The film's success and the conversations it sparked reflect a growing awareness and desire to address these issues more openly and constructively. It also inspires audiences to recognize distorted historical narratives and establish more inclusive and accurate representations. The film's impact extends beyond entertainment, contributing to a broader movement toward racial justice, healing, and a future in which diversity is not just accepted but celebrated.

Avengers: Infinity War (2018) and Avengers: Endgame (2019)[14]

These monumental Avengers narratives are about much more than thrilling battles and stunning visual effects. They offer profound insights into human nature, destiny, the cosmic battle between good and evil, and the quest for meaning in an ever-expanding universe. Each film has been woven as a rich tapestry both semiotically and archetypally. Semiotically, they are rich with symbols, and their respective archetypes resonate with deep theological and existential themes. Both films are replete with timeless themes, including the hero's journey, sacrifice, resurrection, and the eternal battle between light and darkness.

The films reflect our collective anxieties and hopes, projecting a vision of the future where humanity's fate hinges on the actions of heroic and flawed characters. Quintessential heroes such as Iron Man, Captain America, and Thor embody unique virtues and flaws that reflect our own struggles to overcome personal demons and societal challenges. Serving as the shadowy archetype is Thanos, whose godlike power and twisted moral philosophy illustrate the dangers of unchecked ambition and the seductive nature of ultimate power.

Scattered and broken, the *Infinity War* heroes face an enemy whose might and will seem insurmountable. Their dispersion mirrors contemporary society's fragmentation, elusive unity, and looming existential threats. Thanos's quest to balance the universe by eradicating half of all life grotesquely manifests our own fears about scarcity, overpopulation, and environmental degradation. His horrifying solution compels us to confront the complex challenges we face and consider the ethical quandaries they pose.

The name *Thanos* was well chosen to reflect the character who sees genocide as a means to an end. The name abbreviates the Greek word *thanatos*, which means "death."[15] Thanos embodies death and destruction and resonates with the theological and existential understanding of death as the ultimate enemy that brings estrangement and alienation. The character typifies all that seeks to separate us from God, our true selves, our community, creation, and our ultimate purpose.

Infinity War differs from *Endgame* in that the latter offers a narrative of hope, resilience, and collective action. It reminds us that, even in the darkest of times, there is a path forward if we can come together, embrace our vulnerabilities, and tap into the deep reservoirs of human creativity and cooperation. Besides being a thrilling plot device, *Endgame*'s time-traveling aspect presents a symbolic journey through our own history and potential futures that invites us to learn from the past and imagine better worlds.

The film is a riveting culmination of a decade-long journey of loss, resilience, unity, and sacrifice that mirrors the redemptive Christ event. It clearly conveys the idea that victory is not achieved through overwhelming force but through self-sacrifice and love. The Marvel cinematic universe character Tony Stark (Iron Man) eventually embraces these higher values, evolving from a self-absorbed intellectual and technical genius to a kind of Christlike figure who willingly lays down his life for the greater good.

In *Endgame*'s climactic moments, the universe hangs in the balance. Stark's sacrificial act becomes the pivotal moment in the battle against Thanos. His choice to sacrifice his life aligns with the kenotic, self-emptying nature of God expressed in Christ (see Phil. 2:7). His overall journey highlights the essential human need and universal longing for meaningful relationships. His transformation from a solitary figure to one who embraces and cares for his family and friends reflects the Christian understanding of life's purpose found in loving God and neighbor.

From the Christian perspective in which death is not the end but a conquered enemy through the resurrection of Christ, we can see the unfolding mythos of *Infinity War* and *Endgame* as allegories for the great cosmic battle between life and death, light and darkness. Thanos, who embodies death, estrangement, destruction, and nihilism is the antithesis of Christ, who represents life, reconciliation, and the ultimate victory over sin and death. The former seeks to dominate through power; Christ reigns through sacrificial love.

Endgame invites viewers to see their own lives as part of a larger story of redemption and renewal. It reminds us that love is the most powerful force in the universe, and it will bring about the final victory of good over evil.

A Word about *Mythos*

The word *myth* (or *mythos*) evokes many things to many people. For some, it speaks to ancient gods and images from epic tales. For many it alludes to mere fantasy, outdated stories, or baseless narratives. In the current vernacular, the word often cynically denotes ideas that are devoid of any merit or truth.

In reality, *mythos* denotes something far more profound. Myths serve as a crucial means by which humans make sense of their world. They convey a form of truth that is told in metaphorical language to embody universal and timeless truths about human existence, society, and the cosmos—ideas that can be conveyed and understood cross-culturally and across the epochs.

To understand mythos as a form of truth requires us to distinguish it from modern notions of scientific or historical truth. While science and history seek to describe and explain the world in empirical and factual terms, mythos seeks to interpret and give meaning to our existence in a more poetic, narrative form. Both presentations of truth are necessary for a full understanding of the world and our place in it.

Myths are powerful in part because they operate at a level deeper than literal historical fact; they work in the realm of meaning and significance where metaphor, symbolism, and narrative express truths about the human condition that ordinary, factual language struggles to capture. Myths speak to our deepest fears, aspirations, conflicts, and questions. They help us navigate complex psychological and existential terrains, offering insights into the nature of love, power, conflict, and redemption, for example.

Mythos is a vital narrative framework through which humanity through the ages has explored and expressed the deepest truths about itself and the world. Mythos is universal and timeless because it taps into shared aspects of the human experience and explores foundational themes such as creation and destruction, life and death, gods and mortals, heroes and villains. Myths resonate with people from all walks of life because they reflect the universal aspects of being human: our need for meaning, our struggle with mortality, our capacity for love and heroism, and our curiosity about the unknown.

Myths are not static relics of the past; they are ageless, living stories that continue to inspire, challenge, and guide humanity. Myths evolve and adapt as they are retold through generations, taking on new meanings and relevance and demonstrating their intrinsic truth and vitality. They are a testament to the power of story to convey enduring truths about the human spirit.

Seeing Ourselves through Cinematic Myths

The films we sampled invite us to reflect on the nature of power, the importance of choice, and the impact of individual and collective actions on the future. They remind us that while the universe is fraught with danger and uncertainty, it is also a place of possibility and hope. This duality is central to Christian eschatology, which holds that despite the world's brokenness, there is a promised future where God will reconcile all things through Christ—the Alpha and Omega, the beginning and the end, the telos toward which all creation moves.

As followers of Jesus, these stories challenge us to embrace a kenotic, or self-emptying, way of life. Just as Christ emptied himself of all grasping for power and ultimately died on the cross, we are called to let go of our ego, power, and control to serve others and to participate in God's ongoing redemption of the world. This kenotic path is, by its nature, one of vulnerability, compassion, and love. It acknowledges the reality of suffering and evil yet holds steadfastly to the hope of resurrection and new creation.

In a world where the future seems utterly uncertain and rife with hazards, these films echo our deepest human longings. As we engage with such narratives, we are invited to look beyond the immediate to the ultimate future promised in Christ, when every tear will be wiped away and death will be no more. Therefore, these films not only entertain and inspire us but also point us toward the promise that our ultimate hope and destiny are found in the One who is the Beginning and the End.

While these cinematic, mythic experiences mirror our anxieties, hopes, dreams, and complexity, they also awaken in us a longing for the heroes' decisiveness, their ability to effect change, and their unwavering commitment to do what is right. They present a vision of rising to the occasion and confronting evil and adversity with integrity and courage. They remind us that each of us is potentially heroic, having the moral fortitude we admire in them, and cultivating within ourselves their best qualities. They also challenge us to consider what heroism really means in a world that is far from black and white—a world in which even heroes live with measures of ambiguity and fear.

Realizing that such complexity is a fact of life, we can understand why our heroes have evolved. In reality, they have changed with us. They carry the weight of our collective disillusionment and aspirations and are faithful to the nuances of our human experiences. As much as they inspire and sometimes repel us, they are (more or less) us. Yet sometimes, like Superman, they die.

Notes

1. *The Dark Knight*, directed by Christopher Nolan (Burbank, CA: Warner Bros. and Legendary Entertainment, 2008).

2. *Batman v Superman: Dawn of Justice*, directed by Zack Snyder (Burbank, CA: Warner Bros. Pictures, 2016).

3. Fandom Entertainment, "Batman v Superman: 'Stay Down' Clip Official," YouTube video, 0:45, March 17, 2016, https://www.youtube.com/watch?v=gm7FfnuLRjM.

4. TheRFB 09, "Batman v Superman 'It's Time You Learned What It Means to Be a Man' Restored," YouTube video, 1:02, June 28, 2020, https://www.youtube.com/watch?v=_TCuE09EXtQ.

5. XEDITZ, "Batman v Superman: Dawn of Justice (2016)," YouTube video, 0:30, June 25, 2023, https://www.youtube.com/watch?v=h55JFso5kyM.

6. XEDITZ, "Batman v Superman: Dawn of Justice (2016)."

7. *Justice League*, directed by Zack Snyder (Burbank, CA: Warner Bros. Pictures, 2017).

8. *Justice League*.

9. *Wonder Woman*, directed by Patty Jenkins (Burbank, CA: Warner Bros. Pictures, 2017).

10. *Wonder Woman*; "Wonder Woman Quotes," imdb.com, accessed January 8, 2024, https://www.imdb.com/title/tt0451279/quotes/.

11. "Wonder Woman Quotes."

12. In evangelical and fundamentalist circles, a contentious debate lingers regarding the interpretation of biblical texts related to women's roles. Readings that are often promoted seem to reinforce patriarchal norms, neglecting the historical and cultural contexts of the Scriptures. This approach perpetuates gender inequality and suppresses women's

voices and contributions. A more nuanced understanding of these texts requires delving into the historical context, literary genres, and intended audiences of the biblical narratives to glean a more accurate and empowering message.

13. *Black Panther*, directed by Ryan Coogler (Burbank, CA: Marvel Studios and Walt Disney Pictures, 2018).

14. *Avengers: Infinity War*, directed by Anthony Russo and Joe Russo (Burbank, CA: Marvel Studios, 2018); *Avengers: Endgame*, directed by Anthony Russo and Joe Russo (Burbank, CA: Marvel Studios, 2019).

15. Benjamin M. Austin, "Death," in *Lexham Theological Wordbook*, ed. Douglas Mangum (Bellingham, WA: Lexham Press, 2014), Logos Bible Software.

1

Confronting Existential Fear

Even Superman can bleed and die. More than a narrative twist in a popular movie, this is a stark metaphoric truth about our vulnerability, individually and as a culture. So far, the twenty-first century has been rocky. The 9/11 attacks and the war on terror gripped us and altered our sense of reality. More shakings followed in the 2010s and beyond. Global and national events, political turbulence, growing polarization, issues of climate change, humanitarian crises, and other disasters exacerbated our chaos and introduced new challenges.

As lingering issues came to the boil, social movements such as #MeToo and Black Lives Matter began calling for groundbreaking societal change. Then from out of the blue, a deadly cloud swept across the planet, taking millions of lives and rearranging economies. The COVID-19 pandemic energized the fears and inherited traumas buried deep within the collective psyche and reminded every sentient person of how vulnerable we are. Suddenly, we saw what lay buried beneath our conscious awareness: it was the parts of ourselves we preferred to disown—the vulnerable parts that bleed and can die.

As our coverups gave way, our unconscious struggles came to the light. It was as though the steely walls of our hidden chambers had reached the limits of their forbearance and were forced to release what had been pent up for too long. Many people experienced intensified dreams. Some had night terrors. The isolation of lockdowns made us brutally aware of our endemic isolation in our digitally connected but dissociated world.

Predictably yet unexpectedly, an environment of acute uncertainty compelled us to acknowledge our personal limitations and the universal truths of human existence. It is no wonder that Hollywood responded with a slew of superhero films. In search of solace, we turned our collective gaze toward cinematic heroes who offered inspiration in the madness. But now they not only entertained us; they also reflected and even questioned the notion of heroism.

Our long fiery season has stirred our yearning for heroes. Yet we must also recognize the hero within, not by denying our vulnerability but by braving the terrain of our weaknesses. That is where we discover the seed of our strength. Amid the wreckage of our literal and metaphoric battles, we can find resilience, hope, and the capacity to move forward, even as the ground shifts beneath us.

History Repeats Itself

Throwback Thursday, popularly known as #TBT, gained traction on social media a number of years ago as a forum for sharing nostalgic moments. The weekly ritual's fun side is obvious, but our collective desire to revisit the past is psychologically significant. Like a digital scrapbook, #TBT offers us comfort, continuity, and a sense of identity while preserving our reminiscences and inviting us to reflect on our personal growth.

The hero of Throwback Thursday is not Batman or Superman; it is the past. Invariably, we convince ourselves that the "good old days" were our better days. Rarely is that the whole truth. But our memories feel safe and invite us to come together and recapture what we feel we have lost. If only for a moment, they provide a communal escape from the pressures of today.

Whichever heroes we seek, our shared experiences mark the connection between the personal and collective unconscious. Great minds such as Carl Jung and Marion Woodman saw this connection in the archetypal patterns and shared myths that shape our way of understanding ourselves and our world. The patterns are perennial, repeating themselves across the ages in folklore, literature, movies, music, and online rituals.

During the cultural, political, and technological revolutions of the 1980s, an anthemic song emerged—Bonnie Tyler's rendition of "Holding Out for a Hero."[1] The lyrics were a lament for a disappearing class of brave figures who enter the dark places when danger threatens and hope fades. The song's pulsating rhythm and soaring vocals became emblematic of thirty- and fortysomethings like me who felt the weight of midlife complexities. With Cold War fears lingering and our collective disenchantment growing, the song's lyrics echoed the clash between our youthful ideals and our rapidly changing world.

Today, the song stands as a reminder to members of Generations X, Y, Z, and Alpha that every generation battles with uncertainty and hopes to find stability. People from every era desire a hero who can restore hope, courage, and the possibility of redemption. As a powerful expression of a culture in transition, a song can articulate the collective yearning for meaning, direction, and a touch of the extraordinary amid life's ordinary trials.

The song Bonnie Tyler sang also reminds us to take courage in acknowledging our vulnerabilities. Doing so becomes a turning point in our personal narrative. As we mature, the stories to which we cling and the heroes around whom we unconsciously constellate evolve with us and within us, reflecting the light and shadow in our own souls. Ultimately, the promise of life compels us to confront our limitations and other universal truths of human existence. We cannot break the bonds of either until we admit that we are bound.

Heroes and Myth Making

The longing for heroes is embedded in our collective psyche. Whether we seek them in the lyrics of a song or the pages of a comic book, we continue the ancient practice of mythmaking. The thread of mythos that began before antiquity also runs through our world today, tying together all people in the search for meaning and transcendence.

The ancient myths, particularly those of the Greek pantheon, include a bewildering array of deities and other characters that embody vice and virtue together. These complex figures engage in petty squabbles as often as great acts of valor. Their tales were not only entertaining to ancient audiences; they helped people navigate the elusive mysteries of humanity and nature.

These stories have stood the test of time. They remind us that the hope and truth we seek in our heroes is exactly what the generations before us sought. The gods, heroes, monsters, and miracles of the ancient mythological narratives form the foundation of many modern platforms, including DC and Marvel superheroes. The ancient Greeks envisioned their heroes in mesmerizing and troubling ways, much as we do. They attributed to their gods human-like qualities that reflected the best and worst of human nature, much as we do. The gods of Olympus were capricious and unpredictable, petty and jealous, yet grand

and noble, much like our heroes. They were complex and erratic, prone to fits of anger, envy, and desire. (Remember the wrathful, unfaithful king of the gods, Zeus, and his vengeful queen, Hera.) In other words, they were much like the humans who worshipped them.

The Greeks' anthropomorphic portrayals mirrored human behavior in exaggerated ways, which brought the divine into a relatable realm. This approach acknowledged human fears, aspirations, societal norms, and questions about the universe. It also produced cautionary tales and moral lessons that inspired us. Greek heroes, demigods, and mortals also played significant roles. Often at the mercy of the gods, figures such as Hercules, Achilles, and Odysseus embarked on epic quests, fought monstrous creatures, and faced insurmountable odds. Their stories resonated with the ancient audience's understanding of virtue, honor, and the human struggle against capricious gods and fate itself.

The parallels between today's superheroes and these ancient archetypes are self-evident. Contemporary demigods battle evil forces and deal with personal dilemmas that reflect the vices and virtues of the gods. They navigate a world in which distinctions between right and wrong are murky, and the wielding of great power exacts a heavy price. Carrying forward the legacy of the ancient gods and satisfying humanity's age-old fascination with extraordinary beings, our superheroes connect with our deepest fears and desires about the human condition and the nature of the divine.

Myths and Childhood

As a boy reading my coveted comics, I understood the fascination of mythmaking at an unconscious level. When I transitioned from the carefree dreams of youth to adulthood's sobering realities, I realized that no one reaches maturity unscathed. All of us are marked by deeply wounding experiences. Childhood trauma leaves its imprint on the human psyche. When we have been mistreated, abused, or exposed to dysfunction in a family system, we carry residual behavioral and psychological effects into adulthood.[2] Children are virtually defenseless against these harsh realities.

Overwhelming circumstances often cause children to don the cloak of adulthood prematurely, striving to be the heroes they are not yet equipped to be. They embrace an immense sense of responsibility to heal their families and, at some point, the world. Many children respond to their pain with rebellion, impulsivity, and defiance. Some adopt villainous behaviors as coping mechanisms. Others use humor to hide their pain and existential despair.

These diverse responses are symptoms of an underlying vulnerability that demands to be acknowledged and not repressed.[3] By owning our inherent weaknesses, we dismantle our protective facades and discover our yearning to be loved, accepted, seen, heard, and valued. This taking of ownership is a critical step in the journey toward healing and wholeness.

Although everyone enters adolescence and young adulthood with some kind of wounding, we remain unprepared to fully acknowledge our emotional bruises until sometime in our middle years. If we want the truth and desire real freedom, we need to respond to the God who invites us, by the Spirit, to face our vulnerabilities. This is the pathway to growth, and when we are ready, only we can choose to take it.

The journey toward wholeness is not for the faint-hearted, however. Once we admit that we are vulnerable, we need courage to face what we would rather forget. Carl Jung reminds us that "we cannot change anything unless we accept it. Condemnation does not liberate, it oppresses."[4] Avoidance is never a solution. To reintegrate the parts of ourselves that are fragmented, we must confront our past, our fears, and our wounds. Therein is the turning point at which genuine healing becomes possible. Really, the essence of the human condition is the lifelong process of becoming, healing, and transcending.

Laying Bare the Fault Lines

On the path of our shared humanness lie two choices: we can address our fears and failures, or we can flee from them. As long as we choose the latter, our issues become the battleground for future cultural and personal conflicts. Healing and transformation do not result from fleeing trouble but from acknowledging that our vulnerabilities and weaknesses are integral parts of our being. As the apostle Paul made clear, we are made strong in our weaknesses (see 2 Cor. 12:7–10). This paradoxical truth points to the inherent power of finding our resilience in the context of our vulnerability.

My training and pursuit of genuine healing have revealed the wisdom of integrating psychology and theology when dealing with the human condition. Theologians and scholars across various traditions echo the necessity of confronting our shadows while seeking wholeness. Integrating these disciplines allows us to recognize the fault lines that have formed within us. It also fosters a more compassionate understanding of ourselves and our world that supports the mending of our brokenness. I believe this is a viable approach to healing—one that touches the full spectrum of human experience and leads to a more integrated and authentic existence.

Heroes in the Volcano

Our search for archetypal figures who embody the virtues and strengths we desire in ourselves requires us to observe our surroundings. As the pandemic exposed us to widespread mortality, we witnessed within ourselves and others the heroic and the fragile. We faced much more than external threats; each of us encountered our inner worlds, with all our fears and unspoken anxieties.

No wonder we gravitate to cinematic superheroes! They not only provide a brief way of escape, but they infuse us with inspiration. The power of storytelling is enduring. It uplifts, challenges, and unites us during our triumphs and turmoil. Perhaps most importantly, stories keep alive the flame of hope—the belief that despite our difficulties, heroism remains and each of us can help create a better world.

These are deeply emotional realities. In the coming pages, we will delve into the realm of consciousness and the collective unconscious. It is imperative, therefore, to recognize the deep-rooted upheavals that might be simmering below the level of our conscious awareness. These often-hidden disturbances are commonly passed down from generation to generation and remain dormant until certain conditions provoke their eruption. Much like fault lines in the earth's crust, societal and personal events can pierce our consciousness through dreams, night terrors, and cultural conflicts.

That is what the pandemic did. It broke through our "outer crust" and allowed our inner turmoil to surface. At that point, we could no longer deny our vulnerabilities. It was a seismic shift, and it continues to unfold.

Vulnerability and Bonhoeffer

In life's ever-shifting landscapes, the vulnerability that leaps from the shadows demands a response. There have been many tremors since the dawn of this millennium. It is no wonder that buried things—the feelings we have unconsciously repressed, suppressed, or ignored—have now pierced the veil of our denial.

Global resets have that effect. Many Christians would write off such rude awakenings as the work of Satan. Yet I suspect that divine wisdom has ordained a peeling back of our layers so that we can own the fragility that has been woven through humanity since its fall in the garden. The events we have witnessed in recent years have marked our collective consciousness and altered our individual narratives. As a pastor, theologian, and seeker of wisdom, I have witnessed the pain and beauty that coexist in our most vulnerable moments. I have seen them in the tear-filled eyes of those seeking comfort, in the resilient spirits of communities rebuilding from loss, and in the quiet strength of individuals facing their deepest fears. Such moments lay bare the nature of the human condition—not as a flaw to be concealed but as a reminder that we need connection, courage, and hope.

In its essence, vulnerability is about more than our exposure to risk or harm. It is about the decision to face life's uncertainty with an open heart and steadfast spirit. It's about realizing that our limitations and our potential for renewal walk hand in hand—a concept we learn most readily in our adversity.

Dietrich Bonhoeffer, who was martyred by the Third Reich in 1945, seemed to grasp this truth years before his death, but his understanding undoubtedly increased during his time in a concentration camp. Bonhoeffer lived only thirty-nine years, yet he left behind a cache of writings that reveal a deeply transforming, mature vision of God's love and grace.

Among his writings is a sermon from 1932, the year before Hitler came into the fullness of political power. Bonhoeffer wrote the sermon for the baptism of his nephew and addressed this passage from the first epistle of John: "God is love, and those who abide in love abide in God, and God abides in them" (1 John 4:16 NRSVUE). Bonhoeffer compared our human vulnerability to the safety a child enjoys in the love of God.[5] Because "God is love," the beginning and end of life remain cradled in God's hands.[6] "God is love" denotes a divine intrusion into a person's life that defies all that is "visible, understandable, and able to be experienced," setting the foundation of one's life "on the foundation of God's own self" and "beyond all human possibilities."[7]

Part of our fear of being vulnerable involves the idea that we become hapless victims of fate or wickedness. But Bonhoeffer believed that God's love redefines our relationship with fate, because God is "Lord over fate."[8] This is not to say that God's people are exempt from challenges of human existence. But because they belong to the One whom fate cannot bind, they are free to "abide in love."[9]

In facing our human vulnerability and surrendering ourselves to God's love, we embark on a transformative journey that redefines our understanding of strength and weakness and leads us to the essence of what it means to be truly human and flourish in the light of divine grace.

Practicing Resurrection

- In the wake of increasing uncertainty in recent years, in what ways have you sensed once-dormant issues escaping the confines of your unconscious mind and demanding your conscious attention? Describe the effect on your emotions and feelings. Were you tempted to deny the issue, or did you own and attempt to process it? Explain.

- Many children respond to their pain with rebellion, impulsivity, defiance, or futile attempts to don the cloak of adulthood. Does this statement resonate with your childhood experiences, and if so, how? What benefits and costs resulted?

- Dietrich Bonhoeffer lived through one of the most terrifying periods in world history and left us with wisdom about owning uncertainty. How does his view that God is Lord over fate affect your approach to human vulnerability? How does it revise your views? How does it affect your sense of your future?

Notes

1. Bonnie Tyler, "Holding Out for a Hero," track 4 on *Footloose*, Ensign Music, 1984.

2. Shanta R. Dube, "How Childhood Trauma Can Affect Mental and Physical Health into Adulthood," American SPCC, accessed January 13, 2024, https://americanspcc.org/how-childhood-trauma-can-affect -mental-and-physical-health-into-adulthood/?gclid=EAIaIQobChMIj Oj9zcjbgwMVdpxaBR1oWQrfEAAYASAAEgLCXfD_BwE.

3. Valeria Sabater, "The Five Archetypes of Childhood Trauma," Exploring Your Mind, accessed January 13, 2024, https://exploring yourmind.com/the-five-archetypes-of-childhood-trauma/#.

4. C. G. Jung, *Modern Man in Search of a Soul* (San Diego, CA: Harvest, 1933), 234.

5. Dietrich Bonhoeffer, *The Collected Sermons of Dietrich Bonhoeffer*, ed. Isabel Best, trans. Douglas W. Stott et al. (Minneapolis: Fortress Press, 2012), 30.

6. Bonhoeffer, *The Collected Sermons of Dietrich Bonhoeffer*, 30.

7. Bonhoeffer, *The Collected Sermons of Dietrich Bonhoeffer*, 30.

8. Bonhoeffer, *The Collected Sermons of Dietrich Bonhoeffer*, 30.

9. Bonhoeffer, *The Collected Sermons of Dietrich Bonhoeffer*, 31.

2

The Tragic Hero

Fear and anxiety are part of the human experience, and every one of us navigates both in the shadow of the future. There is a passage between the *now* and the *next* that beckons and thrills us. Yet there can be hair-raising moments when the uncertainty of the outcome gives us pause. We long to enter the future that has been intimated and dreamed of, but we find that the crossing of the threshold is a journey all its own—one that reveals and then transforms us.

God's people have taken many such journeys. In the era of the judges, people navigated their fears and anxieties against a backdrop of ethical chaos and the absence of centralized leadership. In an incident that epitomized the nation's depravity, men in the Benjamite city of Gibeah assaulted the concubine of a Levite (see Judges 19). The deed was so vile that it ignited a civil war within Israel, leading to the near-annihilation of the tribe of Benjamin (see chap. 20). The tragedy of Gibeah indelibly stained the tribe's honor and underscored the need for righteous leadership in an era when "everyone did what was right in his own eyes" (21:25).

Within the context of collective shame, the narrative turns to a man of integrity—Kish of Gibeah, a man of valor within the tribe of Benjamin. Despite his city's dark legacy, Kish embodies virtue. His legacy would be significantly shaped by his devoted son, Saul, whose own life was inextricably woven into the tumultuous transition from the judges era to the establishment of Israel's monarchy (1 Sam. 9:1–2).

An Unexpected King

The people of Israel clamored for a king to lead them "like all the nations," rejecting the theocratic rule that had guided them (1 Sam. 8:5). The desire for a king was largely born out of frustration with Samuel's sons, who were corrupt and did not walk in his ways (8:3). Although the request itself reflected a departure from divine guidance, God acquiesced to their demands, setting the stage for Saul's unexpected rise to kingship. Yet even in this seeming diversion, God's sovereignty was not thwarted.

At this time, Saul was already a father to Jonathan and was likely in his late thirties.[1] When some of Kish's donkeys went missing, Kish tasked Saul with their retrieval. The overall sociocultural and historic context of ancient Israel reveals insights into the everyday life and values of the time. For example, donkeys were valuable assets and signs of wealth, being essential for agricultural work and transportation. Because the loss of such animals could negatively affect a family's livelihood, the narrative is driven on one level by very practical concerns.

Also reflected in the story and in Saul's assignment to find the donkeys is the sense of familial responsibility within Israel's patriarchal society. As a son, Saul was expected to obey his father, which he did with profound diligence, honor, and deference.[2] This act of filial piety (especially when juxtaposed with Eli's disobedient and wayward sons, Hophni and Phinehas, and the corrupt sons of Samuel),[3] signals a pivotal shift in the narrative landscape of Israel's leadership. Saul's readiness to heed his father marks him as a figure of potential renewal and hope for Israel, a nation that had suffered from previous generations' failures.

This seemingly mundane mission was imbued with significance and marked the beginning of Saul's transformation from a young Benjamite man of the countryside to the anointed leader of Israel. The search would lead Saul to the prophet Samuel (9:3–10), who would anoint him as the first king of Israel (10:1). A series of providential disappointments, divine encounters, and prophetic revelations would complete Saul's divinely intended transformation.

This kind of narrative was common in biblical and ancient Near Eastern literature. It included the idea of a routine task leading to a significant destiny, illustrating how the divine can manifest in ordinary circumstances. As is typical, symbols are part of the narrative. Here, the donkeys symbolize peace and servitude. The choice subtly foreshadows Saul's initial reluctance to becoming king and his eventual struggle with the responsibilities that kingship entails.

Yet donkeys also carry royal connotations, serving as the mounts of kings in various scriptural accounts.[4] This association adds to Saul's quest a layer of divine irony and foreshadowing: in the commonplace pursuit of lost donkeys, Saul unwittingly enters the sublime position of a future king who would ride donkeys in a manner befitting his newfound royal status.[5] The humdrum search becomes a pathway to destiny. By seeking the ordinary, Saul encounters the extraordinary.

If we wrestle with this ancient text and see beyond the story's surface, the unfolding of God's providential plan for Saul can remind us to hear what the Spirit is saying now—to us. The Saul narrative becomes a metaphor for divine guidance and revelation. Saul's search for "royal beasts" leads him to Samuel the prophet.[6] The ensuing moment of anointing is more than the culmination of Saul's search; it is a testament to the ways in which God's purposes are often revealed in the pursuit of our everyday responsibilities.

Discovering Our Royal Identity

The Saul narrative sheds light on the spiritual quest, suggesting that the path to discovering God's will and our own royal identity in him can begin in the faithful execution of seemingly ordinary tasks. Saul's story becomes a parable of sorts, reminding us that in the kingdom of God, the quest for "a penny" can lead to the discovery of "buried treasure."[7] It challenges us to remain open to the divine possibilities hidden within our daily endeavors and urges us to embrace the obedience and attentiveness that precede the realization of our God-given destinies. This choice places us in a place of creative tension between the known and the unknown, the seen and the unseen.

This is precisely what drives the Saul narrative forward and engages us in the unfolding story. The writer of 1 Samuel brilliantly leads us on the same path as Saul, foreshadowing Saul's quest and his encounter with Samuel, the seer-prophet who will anoint him as king. This meeting is ostensibly coincidental but unmistakably laden with divine intentionality, implying that Saul's destiny is being shaped by forces he does not immediately comprehend.

Saul's intent is to find his father's donkeys. But when he encounters Samuel, his donkey search becomes secondary, and the larger story of Israel's transition to monarchy becomes clear. Nevertheless, the quest for the donkeys echoes other biblical themes of loss, search, and divine guidance. Biblically, it also resonates with the larger story arc in which individuals who are reluctant or see themselves as unworthy are called out of their ordinary lives into roles of great significance.

This story arc is not exclusively Saul's. It is also ours. It points us to a form of resurrection in which we are seen by God in ways that we do not yet see ourselves. When Israel demanded a king, God selected a man who saw himself as less-than—a man fit to search for donkeys but not quite qualified to lead his people. His story resonates with us not only because its writing was divinely inspired but also because we fail to see all that God (and others) see in us. His story is instructive. His search for donkeys was an entrée to the larger divine intent: his discovery of his royal identity. It is to this search that we too are invited.

A Tragic Story

Because it is a human story, Saul's story is not one of unblemished heroism. His reign is characterized by moments of victory and divine favor but also marred by deep-seated insecurities and a lack of confidence in his own capabilities (see 10:22; 15:17–24). Saul's internal struggles, his disobedience to God's commands, and his eventual descent into jealousy and paranoia, seen most vividly in his dealings with David, cast a shadow over his kingship (see 18:8–9; 28:15–19). Saul's tragic trajectory underscores the complexities of leadership and the consequences of personal failings in the face of divine expectations. From his humble beginnings in the search for lost donkeys to his anointment as king and his subsequent downfall, the text presents the existential tension between human ambition and divine will.

Saul's failings remind us that the outward qualities of valor and honor need to be balanced by our submission to God's guidance in humility and faith. Saul's story speaks to the virtues and vices that shape our lives and to the ways in which we look for our leaders to be our heroes. We can see his story through the lens of Aristotle's principles of tragedy and the construction of the tragic plot.[8] Saul's journey embodies many of the elements Aristotle identifies as central to the tragic narrative, particularly the transformation from good fortune to bad that is precipitated not by inherent wickedness but by a tragic flaw.[9]

Much like the tragic heroes Aristotle describes, Saul is a figure of high station who initially finds favor in the eyes of both God and the people of Israel. His honorable search for his father's donkeys providentially leads him to Samuel, who anoints him as Israel's first king. Mirroring the plot structure of other tragedies, Saul's unexpected elevation to royal anointment reveals destiny taking a hand in the protagonist's life.

True to the Aristotelian notion of tragic flaw (*hamartia*), Saul's serial misjudgments and acts of disobedience lead to his downfall. His inability to fully trust God's commands, his impatience, and his jealousy toward David are emblematic of this flaw and portend his decline. Whether the nature of such flaws in tragic heroes is primarily intellectual or moral is a matter of debate.[10] Perhaps it is both. More importantly, the editors of Aristotle's work caution us not to see the protagonist's downfall as a deserved fate but as one precipitated by a critical error or misjudgment, possibly stemming from a character imperfection.[11] Although calamities ensue as a result, the hero's imperfection doesn't necessarily render the hero morally responsible for the ensuing calamities.

Saul's tragic story evokes the emotions of pity and fear that Aristotle sees as central to tragedy.[12] Saul's fall from divine favor invokes our pity because, although his misfortune is linked to his flaws, it seems disproportionate to his initial intentions and virtues. Therefore, the intent is for a holy fear to emerge from our reading of Saul's story. If we read the narrative faithfully, we cannot help but identify with him, realizing that his decisions mirror our own potential for moral failure. His decline is a cautionary tale of how even those chosen and blessed can falter grievously. For all of us, the precariousness of human virtue renders the possibility of downfall ever present.

Of Saul and Us

Saul's life story takes on the trajectory that Aristotle favors: from the search for donkeys to the acceptance of kingship and ultimate demise, the plot moves from happiness to disaster.[13] It is transformed from a simple historical account into a multilayered exploration of themes such as divine providence, the unpredictability of destiny, and the intersection of human agency and divine will. This approach underscores the story's powerful conveyance of spiritual and existential questions, which is accomplished through a deceptively simple search for what is lost and which reminds us that the sacred and heavenly can manifest in life's most predictable everyday aspects.

The story is not a simple moral tale but a rich, multifaceted narrative that explores the weight of leadership, the challenges of obedience, and the impact of personal flaws on one's destiny. Consistent with Aristotle's criteria, Saul's downfall is not the result of outright villainy but of a tragic flaw. This distinction is crucial; it differentiates Saul's story from tales of retribution against evil. Instead, it presents a deeply human portrait of failure and underscores the tragic hero's mix of virtues and flaws.

Saul's journey is not a mere historical narrative; it is a mirror reflecting the complexities of our own inner lives. His story moves beyond the external and invites us to explore the psychological underpinnings that shape our destinies. As flawed people, we can relate to Saul. His descent offers a lens through which to confront our personal and collective struggles. There we meet our anxieties, our existential angst, our unrest in the face of unmet expectations, our perceived inadequacies, our doubts, and our fears.

We know the feeling of being overwhelmed by the roles and responsibilities life seems to thrust on us. We are appalled by Saul's reaction to David's ascent, yet we see him in ourselves. We can attest to our own bouts of panic. If we are honest, we can imagine being driven to violent manifestations of our existential anxiety. Saul reminds us of the inescapable commingling of brokenness and beauty in us all. A passage of Scripture can help us grasp this complexity in Saul and in us:

> Then he brought the tribe of Benjamin near by its families, and the Matrite family was taken. And Saul the son of Kish was taken; but they looked for him, and he could not be found. Therefore they inquired further of Yahweh, "Has the man come here yet?" So Yahweh said, "Behold, he is hiding himself by the baggage." So they ran and took him from there, and he stood among the people. And he was taller than any of the people from his shoulders upward. (10:21–23)

At this point in Saul's life, lots are being drawn to reveal that he is the king-designate. Samuel holds a solemn assembly at Mizpah and delivers a sobering and divine pronouncement.

> Then Samuel called the people together to Yahweh at Mizpah; and he said to the sons of Israel, "Thus says Yahweh, the God of Israel, 'I brought Israel up from Egypt, and I delivered you from the hand of the Egyptians and from the hand of all the kingdoms that were oppressing you.' But you have today rejected your God, who saves you from all your calamities and your distresses; yet you have said, 'No, but set a king over us!' So now, take your stand before Yahweh by your tribes and by your clans." (10:17–19)

From his first prophetic utterance to Eli (3:18), Samuel had faithfully executed his role. Here he reflects on Yahweh's benevolence toward Israel by showcasing a pattern of divine rescue and grace all the way back to the exodus event. Samuel is clear: Israel has rejected the God of exodus events, and his grace, as though he were unable to deliver them from the Philistines. According to Walter Brueggemann, "Israel's desire for a king is understood as a nullification of the saving past and of the God who saves."[14] Israel's insistence on a king represents a breach of trust and gratitude toward Yahweh. From this vantage point, monarchy is not a form of divine provision but a departure from reliance on God.

Despite the grave implications of this rejection and the clear reservations of Samuel and Yahweh, the selection of a king proceeds. Paradoxically, God is committed to honoring Israel's misguided request. The selection by the casting of lots, which seems primitive to us, testifies of a society convinced of God's sovereignty over all human affairs, even those involving governance. For Brueggemann, the juxtaposing of the lots with the earlier mention of the Spirit's anointing of Saul (vv. 9–13) adds layers of divine mystery and sacramentality to the establishment of Saul's kingship.[15] This liturgical process affirms Saul's earlier secret anointing and underscores the tension between divine will and human agency. Saul's public designation as king is fraught with spiritual, psychological, theological, and political complexities but is also marked by a sense of sacred ceremony, affirming God's mysterious workings in establishing Israel's monarchy. We cannot surmise that God has no intent in all of this, nor that he does not care. God indeed cares, and God indeed yearns for his people to trust him. The deep theological undertones and symbolism of this narrative arc invite us to reflect on the nature of divine-human interaction, the cost of human desires that deviate from divine intention, and the unsearchable ways in which God's purposes unfold, even when our own actions seem to contradict his intent.

The Power of Projection

Israel's yearning for a monarch exemplifies the projection of a society's inner fears onto a desired authority figure, revealing timeless psychological patterns that persist to this day. When Israel demanded a king who fit the mold of other nations' kings, they pivoted from faith to fear and exchanged their reliance on the divine for an immediate sense of security. Their choice did not reflect on God; it was a projection cast via their inner brokenness.

A parallel in contemporary culture is the phenomenon of Christian nationalism. Just as Israel sought a king to assuage their fears and secure their place among nations, Christian nationalism responds to perceived threats against cultural and religious identity within the modern state. As an ideology, it attempts to reclaim a sense of control and security by amalgamating faith and national power. It mirrors Israel's ancient desire to legitimize and defend their communal identity by choosing a king.

This parallel invites us to reflect on faith in the public square. It challenges believers to discern between the pursuit of godly justice and the temptation to seek power and security through earthly political structures. It calls us to reevaluate our expectations of security, and it encourages us to trust again in divine sovereignty, regardless of the cultural and political upheaval we face.

What Israel attempted in demanding a king, and what Christian nationalism demands today, are precisely opposite to the practice of resurrection. We cannot resurrect ourselves by mustering our personal or collective power. Resurrection is a divine outcome to which we are invited by grace. Israel's rejection of divine governance rejected this invitation. Instead, it revealed a yearning to metaphorically imprint a human face—a king's face—on the coins of their realm.

Machiel Klerk offers a quote from Jung on projections: "Projections change the world into a replica of one's own unknown face."[16]

Projection is a defense mechanism by which we unconsciously transfer our undesirable feelings, desires, or attributes onto others.[17] These include the emotions and traits that we find incompatible with our way of seeing ourselves. Because they do not fit our carefully edited picture of self, we project them outward onto the world. In doing so, we shape and reshape our perceptions of reality.

Through projection, the external world and the people in it mirror back to us the parts of ourselves that we have disowned. The world we navigate becomes a replica of these unknown or unacknowledged parts. Jung's speaks of the "unknown face" as aspects of self that remain in the shadow, *shadow* being Jung's term for a particular archetype that "represents the 'darker side' of the human psyche, which may comprise anything (e.g., a trait, desire, or emotion, whether positive or negative) that is unacceptable to an individual's conscious ego and as such remains unexpressed and hidden in the unconscious."[18]

By projecting, we alter our understanding and interaction with the world, seeing our hidden traits in other people rather than recognizing them as our own. This mechanism distorts relationships and hinders personal growth. Instead of addressing inner conflicts directly, it externalizes them. In this context, the importance of self-awareness and the journey toward integrating our disowned parts becomes self-evident. But by confronting and reclaiming our projections, we can achieve a more authentic and holistic understanding of who we are, reducing the distortion in our perceptions of others and the world.

Israel's striving to ensure stability, protection, and a cohesive identity caused their aspirations and anxieties to converge on one man. Saul became the embodiment of their highest hopes, a receptacle for their deepest fears, and a perceived escape from their disowned aspects. Imagine if the once king-less nation and the object of its affection— the well-meaning but tragic hero Saul—had instead reclaimed and recognized their projections and accepted the parts of themselves that they tried to deny.

Imagine if we would do the same. The result might be what most human beings still desire: to foster a more genuine and harmonious relationship between our inner selves and our external realities. Instead of passing judgment (which is what the defense mechanism of projection does),[19] we might acknowledge our fears, own our individual and collective flaws, and avoid unending cycles of fragmentation.

In this regard, each of us is like Saul; we are tragic heroes in need of redemption.

Practicing Resurrection

- A series of providential disappointments, divine encounters, and prophetic revelations completed Saul's transformative transition to kingship. Can you describe a specific situation in which God's unexpected but providential plan unfolded in your life? How did the Spirit help you to grasp God's intent? How did you cooperate? How might you have cooperated more readily?

- Saul's story resonates with us, in part because he failed to see what God saw in him. We also fail to see all that God (and others) see in us. In what specific ways has this been your experience? How has your "search for donkeys" led you to the heart of the larger divine plan? How has your royal identity been revealed to you?

- How has the discussion of projection provoked you to examine your heart and your intentions more closely? How might the external world and people in it be mirroring back to you parts of yourself that you have unwittingly disowned? Which aspects of yourself remain in the shadow?

Notes

1. Samuel remained judge over Israel until old age (1 Sam. 8:1), which probably means some thirty years after the battle of Ebenezer. At this point, Israel requested a king and Samuel anointed Saul to be king. Sometime while Saul was pursuing David in the wilderness, Samuel died. Saul reigned for forty years (Acts 13:21) and died at the battle of Gilboa. David, who had been anointed a number of years earlier, became king in Hebron for seven years and six months and then moved to Jerusalem, where he reigned for thirty-three years. The further chronology of 1–2 Samuel is summarized in the chart below, though a number of the ages are admittedly somewhat speculative.

Event	Samuel's Age	Saul's Age	David's Age
Ebenezer	40?	10?	
Request for a king	70	40	
Saul becomes king	70+	40+	
David born	80	50+	1
David anointed	97	67	17
David and Goliath	97	67	17
Samuel dies	105	72	22
Saul pursues David		72–80	22–30
Saul dies at Gilboa		80	30
David reigns in Hebron			30–37
David reigns in Jerusalem			37–70

Peter J. Leithart, *A Son to Me: An Exposition of 1 & 2 Samuel* (Moscow, ID: Canon Press, 2003), 35–37. Unlike other researchers who consider Saul younger, Leithart sees him as a mature man, likely in his forties with a son old enough to serve in the army. Leithart, *Son to Me*, 72–73.

2. Likewise, under Israel's hierarchical social structure, the servant who accompanied Saul was called to assist in furthering the family's economic health.

3. Leithart, *Son to Me*, 72–73.

4. Leithart, *Son to Me*, 72–73.

5. Leithart, *Son to Me*, 72–73.

6. Leithart, *Son to Me*, 72–73.

7. Leithart, *Son to Me*, 72–73.

8. Aristotle, *Aristotle in Twenty-Three Volumes*, trans. W. H. Fyfe (Cambridge, MA: Harvard University Press; London: William Heinemann Ltd., 1932), 23. (page #)

9. Aristotle, *Aristotle in Twenty-Three Volumes*, 23.

10. Aristotle, *Aristotle in Twenty-Three Volumes*, 23.

11. Aristotle, *Aristotle in Twenty-Three Volumes*, 23.

12. Aristotle, *Aristotle in Twenty-Three Volumes*, 23.

13. Aristotle, *Aristotle in Twenty-Three Volumes*, 23.

14. Walter Brueggemann, *First and Second Samuel*, Interpretation, a Bible Commentary for Teaching and Preaching (Louisville, KY: John Knox Press, 1990), 78.

15. Brueggemann, *First and Second Samuel*, 78.

16. Machiel Klerk, "You Are My Mirror and I Am Yours," Jung Society of Utah, April 29, 2016, https://jungutah.org/blog/projection-you-are-my -mirror-and-i-am-yours-2/.

17. *APA Dictionary of Psychology*, s.v. "projection," accessed February 19, 2024, https://dictionary.apa.org/projection.

18. *APA Dictionary of Psychology*, s.v. "shadow," accessed February 19, 2024, https://dictionary.apa.org/shadow.

19. When Jesus said, "Judge not lest you be judged" (Matt. 7:1) and continued speaking in vv. 2–3, he made it clear that such judgment is projection.

3

Recognizing Tragic Flaws

The Godfather film franchise stands as a towering cinematic achievement and a deep exploration of power, loyalty, and the complexities of human nature.[1] At the heart of this epic saga is the character of Michael Corleone, whose journey from reluctant outsider to ruthless patriarch of a criminal enterprise mirrors archetypal narratives like the biblical account of Saul. Michael also begins his journey as a figure of great potential and moral integrity. Although he takes a stance against the family's dealings, he is eventually drawn deep into the violence, betrayal, and moral compromise he once resisted.

Both Saul and Michael Corleone begin their respective narratives standing on the periphery of power, reluctant to assume the roles destiny has in store. Saul, a humble farmer's son, is anointed as Israel's first king. Michael, who recoils at his father's business, finds himself pulled into it after an attempt is made on his father's life. Like Saul, Michael is a loyal son. For Michael, however, that loyalty leads him to accept what once repelled him.

Michael Corleone's deep respect for his father, Don Vito Corleone, is juxtaposed with his initial divergence from the family legacy. The attempted assassination of his father becomes a turning point that exposes Michael's internal struggle: he is torn between his desire for a legitimate life and the pull of familial loyalty and legacy.

The pull is powerful. Don Vito's influence on Michael is formidable, shaping his understanding of power, leadership, and morality despite his conscious resistance. He values his father's principled approach to leadership, which emphasizes respect, loyalty, and a sense of justice—albeit within the criminal context. These qualities set a standard to which Michael aspires. Paradoxically, however, Michael's leadership methods diverge from his father's more measured approach. Instead of reflecting his earlier moral ideals, Michael's methods lean toward ruthlessness and isolation. This deviation underscores his attempt to both preserve the Corleone legacy and redefine it in his own image.

Legacy, Descents into Darkness, and Tragic Flaws

Saul's relationship with his father, Kish, is not as detailed as the relationship between Michael and Don Vito Corleone. Yet it is equally as pivotal. Both sons become tragic heroes, and both their lives suggest the tension between legacy and personal destiny and between personal intent and paternal expectations. Unlike Michael Corleone, who actively steps into his father's world in order to protect the family, Saul is thrust into leadership by divine selection. In this regard, Saul's acceptance of a new role is more passive and reluctant than Michael's and more directed by divine and societal forces.

These complicated and diverse dynamics reveal how father-son relationships can propel individuals toward paths that both fulfill and betray their original intent. To understand these relationships requires a look into the tragic hero's psyche, particularly in uncovering the layers of loyalty, identity, and moral conflict that drive their actions. Both the parallels and contrasts between Michael and Saul expose the burdens of legacy and the profound impact of familial bonds on individual destiny, both of which can portend darker-than-intended outcomes.

At the crux of both sons' stories is the gradual descent into the very darkness they sought to avoid. Saul's insecurities and disobedience to divine commandments signal the beginning of his unraveling, which culminates in jealousy and paranoia toward David, whom Saul perceives as a threat to his throne. Michael's descent is marked by a series of ruthless decisions that seem to him necessary in protecting the family. But each choice leads him further from his moral convictions and deeper into crime and corruption.

Both men have tragic flaws. Saul's lack of trust in God's guidance contributes to his growing fear and jealousy. Michael masks his pursuit of power and control with claims of protecting his family. Both men's flaws are defining characteristics that precipitate their respective downfalls, including their utter isolation and disconnection from their communities, families, and themselves. Saul's reign ends in despair, rejection from God and his people, and a brutal death on the battlefield. Michael achieves unparalleled power but finds himself alone and haunted by the ghosts of his decisions. The man who set out to protect his family ends up losing their love and respect.

What Was Saul's Reluctancy Really About?

When we consider Saul's sudden elevation to kingship and the immense pressures of leadership and military threats, it seems that he most likely wrestled with significant levels of anxiety and stress. Modern psychology would recognize this as situational anxiety, potentially escalating to chronic stress that could lead to what is known today as generalized anxiety disorder due to the ongoing demands of his role.[2]

Anxiety and Familial and Tribal Background

Saul's background in the aristocracy of the tribe of Benjamin, provides perhaps a first layer of context for his anxiety. We have discussed the tribe's tumultuous history, internal strife, and conflict with other tribes (see Judges 19–21). This checkered history may have contributed to a familial and tribal environment characterized by heightened vigilance, insecurity, and potential anxiety about social standing and security.

Mention of the lost donkeys in 1 Samuel 9 can be seen as a metaphor for the larger existential uncertainties and responsibilities that Saul's family navigated. Approached semiotically, the task of finding the donkeys could symbolize the broader challenges of maintaining and securing one's place in a volatile sociopolitical landscape. Saul's concern over his father's worry over the donkeys could indicate an acute awareness of his familial obligations as they relate to family stressors.

Anxiety and Sudden Elevation to Kingship

Saul's sudden elevation to the throne of Israel—a role that had no precedent in the nation—is a drastic transition that would naturally induce significant stress and anxiety. The abruptness of the change exacerbated the usual weight of leadership, requiring Saul to discover ways of uniting the fractious confederation of tribes under his sole monarchic rule. The expectations for leadership, the ongoing military conflict (particularly with the Philistines), and the need to establish an entirely new political structure would have produced significant stress levels, even for a man more secure and confident than Saul.

Spiritual and Social Expectations

Saul's role was not only purely political; it was deeply spiritual. Ancient Israel's king was seen as the representative of Yahweh himself. Beyond any administrative and political requirements, he was tasked with upholding religious duties and leading the people in their adherence to God's covenant with them. This spiritual dimension added a layer of anxiety, knowing that his failure in this realm could be seen as jeopardizing the favor of God, on which their very success was believed to depend.

Impostor Syndrome

The episode described in 1 Samuel 10:20–23 shows Saul hiding among the baggage as the tribes are casting lots to seal his selection as king. His emotional and psychological response to this momentous occasion could be interpreted in terms of what today's psychologists call impostor syndrome,[3] a term first identified in 1978 by psychologists Pauline Clance and Suzanne Imes.[4] The term describes a psychological pattern of doubts surrounding a person's accomplishments. This pattern includes the persistent, internalized fear among competent people of being exposed as frauds.

Impostor syndrome is not an officially recognized mental disorder in the *Diagnostic and Statistical Manual of Mental Disorders* (DSM-5), but it is acknowledged as a specific form of intellectual self-doubt. Individuals who experience impostor syndrome often attribute their success to luck or claim it has resulted from deceiving others into believing they are more intelligent or competent than they believe themselves to be. This syndrome can affect people regardless of their social status, work history, skill level, or degree of expertise.

Saul's effort to secret himself even as he is being called to the throne would seem to be consistent with impostor syndrome for several reasons:

- *Feelings of unworthiness:* Saul's hiding suggests that he feels unworthy of the throne. Despite being chosen by divine decree through the prophet Samuel, Saul seems to have felt inadequate for the responsibilities and expectations of kingship.

- *Fear of exposure:* Saul's hiding could suggest that he feared having his perceived unfitness for the role recognized by others. This fear is not necessarily rational but often exists, even among those who are highly capable. It is a hallmark of impostor syndrome.

- *Avoidance behavior:* Individuals with impostor syndrome often avoid situations that are crucial to their success because their present fear of being exposed as incompetent is greater than their fear of possibly undermining their future success.

The scriptural narrative does not explain Saul's thought processes. However, viewing his actions through the lens of impostor syndrome can provide a framework for understanding his behavior. I suspect it is more than mere shyness or humility and is instead a deeper psychological struggle with self-perception and the fear of inadequacy.

These perceptions might have been exacerbated by the suddenness of his rise to the throne. Saul was accustomed to a relatively obscure existence and was catapulted to the least obscure position in all of Israel. I would suggest that considering Saul's behavior in relation to the impostor syndrome can illuminate his character and the challenges he faced while highlighting the universality of such psychological experiences across time and cultures.

It must be stated that use of the term *impostor syndrome* is now trendy,[5] and research is ongoing. But the fundamental concept describes a very human experience and provides a bridge between ancient scriptural narratives and contemporary psychological concepts and fosters a more empathetic view of Saul's reign and failings. This brings both his humanity and kingship into sharper relief while humanizing a man who is too often viewed in a purely historical or theological light.

Depression

Paying careful attention to Saul's reign, particularly the episodes of his despondency and the therapeutic effect of David's harp playing (see 1 Sam. 16:23), we see evidence to suggest that Saul may have experienced periods of depression. His psychological state, behavioral symptoms, erratic behavior, and emotional distress in his later years coincide with contemporary understandings of major depressive disorder and lesser depressive disorders.[6]

Present in the story is a pattern of mood swings, irrational anger, jealousy, and a deep despair. These manifestations can be seen in his interactions with David, including his desire to kill David. We also see that David's harp playing brings solace to Saul when the tormenting spirit came upon him. David would play the harp, Saul would feel better, and the evil spirit would leave him. This suggests that Saul's despair was recognized by those around him. The use of music in ancient times is also known to modern psychology as a method of reducing stress, anxiety, and symptoms of depression.

Saul's symptoms, which align with modern diagnostic criteria for depressive disorders,[7] include the following:

- *Persistent sad, anxious, or "empty" mood:* Saul's despondency suggests a deep sadness that affected his ability to function as king.
- *Feelings of hopelessness or pessimism:* Saul's actions, especially in the latter part of his reign, reflect a sense of hopelessness regarding his kingship and legacy.
- *Irritability and restlessness:* Saul's irrational and even violent behavior toward David can suggest extreme irritability and agitation.

- *Changes in appetite and sleep patterns:* Although not explicitly mentioned, Saul's overall erratic behavior could imply disturbances in other areas of functioning, such as sleep and appetite (common to those who suffer depressive disorders).

As is true regarding other aspects of his pain, our attempts to understand Saul's despondency and erratic behavior help us read the story with far more empathy. Such psychological interpretation considers the immense pressures and challenges he faced, both internally and externally. This perspective does not diminish the historical or theological significance of Saul's story but instead enriches it. This approach offers further insight into the human condition and Saul's suffering, as recorded in the biblical narrative.

An overview of Saul's story reveals other behaviors that are indicative of psychological struggles.

Paranoia

Saul's interactions with David and his own son, Jonathan (see 1 Sam. 20:30–33), portray aspects of paranoia as it is understood today. This pattern is crucial to understanding Saul's complex character and tragic trajectory. Clinically, his paranoia manifested as irrational suspicion and mistrust that often led to insufficiently founded assumptions of conspiracy or betrayal.[8]

Paranoia is associated with a range of psychiatric conditions, including paranoid personality disorder, schizophrenia, and, in some cases, mood disorders with psychotic features. It is characterized by intense anxiety or fear (often to the point of delusion) that causes affected individuals to erroneously believe that they are being persecuted or conspired against.[9]

Saul's apparent paranoia manifested in the following ways, some of which also indicate other psychological issues:

- Intense jealousy and fear of David, despite David's loyalty
- Attempts on David's life based only on Saul's distorted perceptions of David's intentions
- Unfounded distrust of his son Jonathan, whom he suspects of conspiring with David (see 20:30–33)

Diagnosing paranoia requires careful clinical evaluation.[10] One of the primary challenges in diagnosing the condition is the subjective nature of the individual's experiences and beliefs. Also, those who experience paranoia may be reluctant to seek help or may distrust mental health professionals. Obviously, the intent here is not to diagnose Saul from afar but to read the text with a degree of sensitivity that does diminish or mischaracterize his apparent suffering. From that vantage point, we can see in Saul's decline signs of this psychologically painful condition.

Impulse Control Issues

Saul's sudden, rash acts of violence indicate impulse control issues.[11] Such manifestations demonstrate the failure to resist temptations, urges, or impulses that may bring harm to oneself or others. Instances of Saul's lack of impulse control include the following:

- His hurling of a spear at David (18:11) as an emotional and unreasoned response
- His ordering the priests and other inhabitants of Nob to be massacred (22:19), without deliberation or regard for either justice or morality

Saul's impaired impulse control had grievous consequences for him personally and for the kingdom of Israel. It contributed to his isolation, the loss of trust among his followers, and the deterioration of his relationship with God. Politically, it led to instability and violence, undermining his authority and contributing to his downfall.

In noting these actions, the text may be drawing our attention to the importance of wisdom, self-control, and the consideration of consequences in leadership. It may also help us understand why we do the things we do[12] so that we develop self-awareness and emotional self-regulation. Surely, the text also recommends our compassion for a man who was so pained by life and even the blessings God bestowed on him.

Saul's sudden acts of violence invite us to explore the concept of impulse control issues in a theological, historical, and psychological context. These incidents reflect the broader theme of the human condition and our all-too-human struggle with impulse control and its implications for personal and social well-being. Saul's behavior invites personal reflection on our part into the nature of impulse control issues and their impact on our lives, highlighting the timeless relevance of these psychological concepts and the importance of self-awareness and emotional self-regulation in navigating the complexities of human emotions and actions.[13]

An "Evil Spirit from the Lord"

Without contemporary psychological assessments and considering the historical and cultural context, to diagnose Saul based on modern criteria is at best speculative. In addition, while modern psychology explores childhood experiences in assessing adult behaviors, we have little information about Saul's early life. Thus, we cannot attribute his struggles to specific childhood traumas or dynamics.

However, we know for certain that Saul was being tormented by an "evil spirit from the Lord" (16:14 NRSVUE). This presents a complex intersection of ancient theological concepts and contemporary understanding of psychological phenomena. To fully grasp the narrative requires an understanding of the ancient worldview, the theological interpretations that have evolved over centuries, and how these perspectives differ from modern psychological analysis.

In the ancient worldview and scriptural interpretation, the spiritual and material realms were often seen as closely interconnected, with the actions of divine beings directly influencing human affairs and individual well-being. The description of Saul's distress as an "evil spirit from the LORD" would have been understood as a manifestation of divine displeasure or a test rather than an indication of moral failure on God's part. Ancient readers would not have seen this manifestation as a literal demonization, in the way contemporary readers might interpret it.

When the Scripture speaks of an "evil spirit from the LORD," it does not suggest that God is malevolent. Instead, it expresses a theological perspective that sees all events in the cosmos, whether positive or negative, as falling within the purview of divine sovereignty. This acknowledges God's ultimate authority over creation without necessarily implying direct divine causality for evil acts or conditions.

From the perspective of theological interpretations and the nature of God, theologians and scholars have long wrestled with texts that attribute challenging or negative experiences to the direct intervention of God. This includes the concept of an "evil spirit from the LORD" tormenting Saul. Key in these discussions is the nature of God as fundamentally good, just, and merciful.

Doctors of the church and other theologians have often interpreted such passages allegorically or as pedagogical tools, designed to teach about the consequences of turning away from God's will or the trials that can lead to spiritual growth and renewal. They caution against a literalist interpretation that would directly attribute evil actions or intentions to God.

Meanwhile, contemporary psychology, based in empirical research and scientific methodology, does not engage with supernatural explanations of psychological states. Thus, Saul's distress might be analyzed in terms of mental health conditions, including the ones already discussed. This approach does not diminish the spiritual or theological dimensions of human experience but operates within a different analytical framework focused on the mind and behavior.

Understanding Saul's experience requires us to integrate these various perspectives. The description of Saul's torment by an "evil spirit from the LORD" then serves as a bridge between ancient theological concepts and contemporary understandings of human distress. It challenges us to explore the depths of scriptural interpretation and the breadth of human psychology, recognizing the value of each while acknowledging their distinct views of the human condition.

In the broadest sense, we know that Saul suffered very human afflictions. His torment reminds us that we, too, are human, and even the heroes among embody both beauty and brokenness.

Practicing Resurrection

- The stories of King Saul and Michael Corleone seem larger than life. Yet they signify down-to-earth experiences. How have specific events revealed tragic flaws in your life? How did your very human missteps lead to forms of isolation and disconnection from your community, family, and or yourself?

- Describe an apparently positive situation or outcome that left you feeling like an impostor. What might have triggered a sense of unworthiness or inadequacy? How well-founded was your fear of having your perceived unfitness exposed? How did this concern hinder or help you in the long run?

- There is a difference between accepting personal responsibility and expecting perfection in yourself and others. Saul, for example, faced immense pressures and internal and external challenges that affected his reign as king. Experiences in your life may have contributed to outcomes that seem less than heroic. How might reading the Saul narrative in a more open-hearted, less judgmental way inform your approach to your own imperfections?

Notes

1. *The Godfather*, directed by Francis Ford Coppola (Los Angeles: Paramount Pictures, 1972), https://www.imdb.com/title/tt0068646/?ref_=nv _sr_srsg_0_tt_7_nm_1_q_the%2520godfa.

2. "Generalized Anxiety Disorder (GAD)," Johns Hopkins Medicine, accessed February 19, 2024, https://www.hopkinsmedicine.org/health /conditions-and-diseases/generalized-anxiety-disorder#:~:text=GAD %20means%20that%20you%20are,money%2C%20family%2C %20or%20work.

3. Sanne Feenstra et al., "Contextualizing the Impostor 'Syndrome,'" NIH National Library of Medicine, accessed February 19, 2024, https://www .ncbi.nlm.nih.gov/pmc/articles/PMC7703426/.

4. Feenstra et al., "Contextualizing the Impostor 'Syndrome.'"

5. Leslie Jamison, "Why Everyone Feels Like They're Faking It," *New Yorker*, February 6, 2023, https://www.newyorker.com/magazine/2023 /02/13/the-dubious-rise-of-impostor-syndrome#:~:text=scale"%20for %20researchers%20to%20license,Clance%20and%20Imes%20never %20imagined.

6. "Depression (Major Depressive Disorder)," Mayo Clinic, accessed February 20, 2024, https://www.mayoclinic.org/diseases-conditions /depression/symptoms-causes/syc-20356007.

7. "Major Depression," Johns Hopkins Medicine, accessed February 19, 2024, https://www.hopkinsmedicine.org/health/conditions-and -diseases/major-depression#:~:text=Loss%20of%20interest%20in %20almost,agitation%2C%20increased%20restlessness%2C%20and %20irritability.

8. "Paranoia," Mind, accessed February 19, 2024, https://www.mind.org.uk /information-support/types-of-mental-health-problems/paranoia/about -paranoia/.

9. "Paranoia," Better Health Channel, accessed February 20, 2024, https://www.betterhealth.vic.gov.au/health/conditionsandtreatments/paranoia.

10. "Paranoia," Healthline, accessed February 20, 2024, https://www.healthline.com/health/paranoia#diagnosis.

11. "Impulse Control Disorders," Cleveland Clinic, accessed February 20, 2024, https://my.clevelandclinic.org/health/diseases/25175-impulse-control-disorders.

12. Catalina E. Kopetz, Jacqueline I. Woerner, and Julia L. Briskin, "Another Look at Impulsivity: Could Impulsive Behavior Be Strategic?," accessed February 19, 2024, https://www.ncbi.nlm.nih.gov/pmc/articles/PMC8168538/.

13. "What Is Emotional Self-Regulation and How Do You Develop It?" Healthline, accessed February 19, 2024, https://www.healthline.com/health/emotional-self-regulation.

4

Abiding and the Practice
of Resurrection

In the vast landscape of the human mind are heroes who shape destinies with the force of their will and strength. Among them are the tragic figures of ancient lore who teach us about the delicate balance between greatness and downfall. Within the many archetypes, a certain kind of heroism is particularly resonant. It is not the stuff of otherworldly battles but of the inner quest for truth, authenticity, and freedom.

Truman as True Man

When it comes to the inner quest for truth, Truman Burbank is just such a hero. The protagonist of *The Truman Show*[1] is an everyman or awakening hero whose story develops in the confines of an ordinary world veiled in illusion. Truman's journey moves from the unexamined life of Seahaven to the precipice of the unknown, where the essence of freedom and authenticity mirrors the spiritual and existential awakenings that beckon each of us. Truman doesn't leap from the pages of a comic book or the tragic ancient tale. He represents the potential to confront the illusions that bind each of us. His life urges us to question, seek, and step into the light of truth, however daunting the passage might be.

Truman's life epitomizes the ordinary. He lives in routine and the familiar comfort of home. He is relatable because his experience is universal. His initial ignorance of his situation mirrors our own unexamined lives. He is constrained by societal norms and unchallenged beliefs. At the start of his journey, Truman embodies the innocence and oblivion that are ubiquitous in a world carefully crafted to keep people unaware of its true nature.

Truman gradually realizes and questions his reality, thus portraying the awakening process by which we learn to see beyond the surface of our own lives. His heroism is fueled by an unwavering quest for truth and the innate sense that something is amiss in his world. Despite the comfort and safety his ignorance offers, Truman courageously rejects falsehood and complacency. His journey of self-discovery and transformation is both literal and metaphorical, signifying the move from the darkness of deception into the light of awareness. His transformation is not achieved through external battles but through his inward awakening and brave confronting of his fears.

The climax of Truman's journey is his decision to exit the artificial world of the show. This is his ultimate act of heroism, a leap of faith into the unknown and his liberation from illusion. Truman's exit is a powerful metaphor for the embrace of authentic existence and the spiritual and psychological journey toward freedom and, in a sense, to what Maslow called "self-actualization."[2] Unlike the superheroes of the DC and Marvel universes, Truman possesses no extraordinary powers. He faces no larger-than-life adversaries or epic battles. Instead, his heroism is seen in his capacity for growth, his willingness to question norms, and his commitment to authenticity. His story declares that heroism can be found in the courage to confront the truth of one's existence and choose authenticity over illusion, even when choosing leads to the unknown.

Truman, Meet Saul

Unlike Saul, whose biblical narrative presents a tragic hero headed for his downfall, Truman's story is a narrative of hope. Truman embodies the potential for every person to become a hero in his or her own journey through the power of awareness, choice, and resilience. His story points out the potential for transformation that lies within us as image-bearers. Its inclusive and accessible model of heroism springs from the realities of the human condition and the universal quest for meaning.

Saul's profound struggles and failures are also part of the human condition. In the landscape of our faith, however, we know that when the promise of the Incarnate One illuminates our path, no story ends in darkness. It is in Christ that we find the conquest of all that has conquered us. That is the conquest that breaks the chains of despair and defeat. It is where the divinely intended journey toward full humanness begins anew. Saul's life matters to God and needs to matter to us. So let us remember that the Jesus story does not end at the precipice of our faltering. It advances toward a horizon where grace outshines the shadows and God's healing and sanctification beckon us forward. If we cannot mourn for Saul and Jonathan as David did, our own need for humanness is showing. The truth is, we are ever on a journey to becoming fully alive in the image of the One who calls us by name.

As we traverse the chapters of our own lives, may we, like Truman, step out into the unknown and embrace the *kairos* moments that awaken us from slumber. These appointed times are connected to the purpose and plan of God. They arrest us, capture our attention, and remind us that he is always present, working in us, through us, and for our good. May they challenge us to confront the haunted houses of our souls and guide us further into the light of truth. As the paths of individuation and spiritual awakening converge, may we realize that heroism lies not in the grandiosity of our deeds but in the courage to face the truth and to walk, however imperfectly, toward the dawn of a new life in Christ.

Becoming Awake

In today's fast, chaotic world, societal shifts and technological advancements continuously redefine the fabric of daily life. The pathways through our information overload, polarizing narratives, success orientation, and search for validation have never been more daunting. This landscape makes our awakening from spiritual and psychological slumber more pressing than ever. Here the journey toward consciousness and intentional living gains importance and offers clarity amid the noise.

What I am sharing is an invitation to awaken from the sleep of death and to arise, for Christ will shine on us and guide us, not as the unwise but as the wise who redeem the time. The days ahead, however dark they might seem, hold the promise of transformation and the hope of glory. As we traverse the landscape of our individual and collective lives, we need to ask ourselves whether we might be walking, however unwittingly, through a metaphorical sleep of death.

Ephesians 5:13–16 urges us, "But everything exposed by the light becomes visible—and everything that is illuminated becomes a light. This is why it is said: 'Wake up, sleeper, rise from the dead, and Christ will shine on you.' Be very careful, then, how you live—not as unwise but as wise, making the most of every opportunity, because the days are evil."

There is a bit of Saul in all of us. When read carefully, his narrative holds a mirror to our unconscious ways living. It reflects our unexamined beliefs and unacknowledged fears. It sees the desires that can mistakenly define our lives. Like Saul, we are prone to quests for power and validation and to losing ourselves in a slumber of sorts. We too can slip into a place where our actions are no longer guided by awareness but are reactions to the fears and desires we fail to confront. We too can submit ourselves to routines and the comfort of the familiar. We can unconsciously slip into autopilot and cease to live as fully awake beings.

To awaken from our spiritual and psychological slumber, we need to expose hidden corners of our lives to the light. Like Truman, we have to dare to ask questions about our unchallenged beliefs. We need to acknowledge the silent drivers—the fear and misguided desires that commandeer our lives. I am not suggesting a process of casting judgment on ourselves; I am suggesting that we embrace the transformative power of awareness.

The light that Ephesians speaks of isn't just a metaphor for clarity; it's a reference to the illuminating presence of Christ in our lives. Allowing this light to shine on the parts of ourselves we've kept in the dark not only reveals but also transforms them. What was once hidden becomes a beacon pointing toward a more conscious and integrated way of living. This journey from slumber to vibrancy is about making the most of every opportunity, not in the sense of productivity, but in the richness of experience and depth of connection with ourselves, with others, and with the triune God.

If you reflect on the call, "Wake up, sleeper, rise from the dead" (Eph. 5:14), you have to consider what it means for you. How might you be sleepwalking through life? What aspects of your existence need the transformative light of Christ to shine on them? Awakening is not a one-time event but a continuous process of growth, learning, and transformation. The days may be fraught with challenges, but in your awakening, you find the wisdom to navigate them with grace and purpose. Saint Paul is inviting all of us to embrace the opportunities with readiness, having cultivated a mindset and spirit that allow us to capture moments from the inside out.

Just as Truman broke free from his Seahaven, we can break free from our places of slumber. We must confront and overcome the prevailing trends that challenge our spiritual journey. As difficult as it might be to acknowledge them, we cannot remain oblivious to their impact. If we choose comfort over awareness, we risk missing out on living the resurrection life in Christ.

Pop Culture, Pop Practices

The reticence toward spiritual disciplines, spiritual practices, and genuine spiritual formation within the "popular" church is significant. Several factors are in play, including broader cultural trends and contemporary perceptions of spirituality. In this regard, we owe it to ourselves to understand the times. Otherwise, we will not know what to do.

Pop culture prioritizes instant results and quick fixes that clash with the slow, deliberate nature of spiritual disciplines. Practices like Scripture meditation, fasting, and deep inductive study of the sacred text demand time, patience, and persistence. The current shift toward prioritizing emotional and experiential payoffs often comes at the expense of disciplines that require more effort and provide longer-term growth. We are drawn to profound spiritual experiences but often undervalue the foundational work that disciplines require.

This is largely due to infiltration of the consumer culture in the church. As consumers rather than participants, we reduce spiritual disciplines to commodities or services that we choose or reject based not on what leads to spiritual growth but on what our personal preferences happen to be. There's also a misconception that spiritual disciplines might restrict personal freedom or are legalistic. This also occurs because of our misunderstanding. We overlook the liberating aspects of disciplines and miss the deeper experience of genuine, cross-shaped, spiritual freedom. The absence of visible, accessible examples of these practices contributes to their neglect, as does a lack of vigilance against the individualistic ethos of our contemporary culture. When faith becomes purely personal and privatized, the communal aspects of spiritual formation—worship, the sacraments, confession, and fellowship—become undervalued.

The omnipresence of technology and social media has created a landscape of distraction. With distraction as our comfort zone, engaging in reflective, contemplative practices that require uninterrupted attention and silence is harder than ever. Spiritual disciplines challenge us to confront and step out of our comfort zones. But in a culture that prioritizes the avoidance of discomfort, the challenging aspects of spiritual growth can be less appealing. It seems evident that fostering deep, disciplined spiritual growth and formation will require us to rely on God. After all, Jesus said, "I am the vine, you are the branches; he who abides in Me and I in him, he bears much fruit, for apart from Me you can do nothing" (John 15:5).

Active Abiding

Jesus's call for us to abide in him is not an invitation to passive reliance. He is directing us to actively engage in a life rooted in communion with him and his Father, by the Spirit. We ignore his call to our own spiritual detriment and malnourishment. The life of abiding is the bedrock of spiritual growth and formation. It necessitates an internal recalibration of mind, heart, and will, aligning them with the divine presence and action within us.

Abiding in Christ requires a fundamental transformation of the mind, a deliberate shift from worldly patterns of thought to a mindset steeped in the truths of Scripture and the realities of Christ's cross-shaped kingdom. It means adopting a Christ-centered (or cruciform) perspective that informs our understanding, decisions, and perceptions. This allows the Spirit of God to impart God's wisdom from the inside, shaping our thoughts and actions.

The human heart, which is often described as the seat of our desires, also includes the deep, less-than-conscious interior domains that are involved in the process of transformation. Consider what Paul says in Ephesians 5:13: "Everything exposed by the light becomes visible—and everything that is illuminated becomes a light." The Spirit ever searches our hearts and minds, both at the unconscious depths and at the conscious level (see Jer. 17:10; Ps. 139:23–24; Rom. 8:27). To abide in Christ is to let our hearts be captured by the love of God so that our deepest desires become aligned with his. This involves cultivating a love for God that surpasses all else, letting our affections be guided by the Holy Spirit, and allowing our lives to reflect the fruit of the Spirit.

As we abide in God, we also surrender our will to God's purposes. This act is essential to spiritual growth and maturity and involves a continuous journey of yielding to God's larger eternal purpose, acknowledging that we find true fulfillment only there. It is a challenging journey, however. Even for believers indwelt by the Holy Spirit, the human will retains a propensity to resist, delay, and outright defy God's direction through

- procrastination in responding to God's call,
- reluctance to relinquish personal desires or comforts, and
- sluggishness in our commitment to spiritual disciplines and practices that foster growth and transformation.

The inherent tension within our will pulls us between our desires and God's and highlights the importance of mindful vigilance in our spiritual journey. Healthy self-awareness, rooted in the very practice of the presence of God, makes us more aware of this internal resistance and leads us to acknowledging our need for his grace to overcome it. It involves a moment-by-moment decision to trust that his ways are always higher than ours, favoring our ultimate good and his glory.

The role of the Holy Spirit is crucial in this process. While our will may be dilatory, the Spirit within us works to convict, guide, and empower us to overcome our deeply engrained habits of being. Through the Spirit's prompting, we are reminded of the beauty of God's will, the joy of obedience, and the peace that comes from living in harmony with God's desires for our lives. The Spirit also equips us with the fruit of self-control and patience, enabling us to resist the immediate gratification of our own will and to wait on the Lord's timing. We can also take practical steps to yield to God's purposes. Our depth of engagement with the sacred text, prayer, and community accountability recalibrates our desires and decisions. These practices are not burdens but channels of grace through which we are continually reminded of God's love, mercy, and sovereignty.

Ultimately, surrendering our will to God is an act of worship and recognition of God's absolute goodness, wisdom, and authority. By choosing to lay our all on the altar, we participate in God's larger story of redemption and restoration in the world. This act of surrender, though challenging, leads us into a deeper relationship with God, where we discover the true freedom and real joy.

The Struggle with Surrender

Both King Saul and Truman Burbank struggle in aligning personal will with a higher calling. Saul's actions often reflect a prioritization of his personal judgment and desires over divine instructions, as his unlawful sacrifice and his disobedience in the matter of the Amalekites show (1 Sam. 13:8–14; 15). His dilatory and disobedient choices ultimately result in God rejecting him as king. The struggle for Saul is not only with external enemies but primarily with his internal resistance to divine sovereignty. He found it difficult to sublimate his personal ambition and fear to his trust in God's wisdom.

The very different and fictional character of Truman reveals an internal conflict of agreeing with the actual truth. Truman inhabits an artificial world in which the show's creator, Christof, manipulates his actions and choices. However, as Truman begins sensing the artificiality of his surroundings, he questions and ultimately rejects the life script he was handed for the sake of discovering authentic reality. Doing this means forfeiting the comfort and security of his known world, overcoming the inertia of a manufactured existence, and managing his fear of the unknown. Truman's decision to escape is the ultimate act of surrendering his will and satisfying his need truth and freedom.

The struggle to surrender is universally human. The struggle requires mindfulness, courage, and a willingness to confront the unknown. Through abiding, we learn to live not just in the moment but within the eternal, transforming our understanding of presence, choice, and the pursuit of a life fully aligned with God's will. This commitment asks us to place our trust in the belief that God's intentions are rooted in goodness, and that the essence of true liberty and fulfillment is in yielding to His invitation to live by faith. We will explore this concept more in a forthcoming chapter, but for the present moment, it's crucial to emphasize two fundamental truths:

- God finds joy in a relationship characterized by faithfulness. The essence of our walk with God is not found in mere ritual or adherence to rules but in a dynamic relationship fueled

by faith. Without faith, it is impossible to please God, for he
desires his children to trust him and step forward in faith,
recognizing his sovereignty and love (see Heb. 11:6).

- Faith manifests through obedience. Genuine faith is not passive. It acts. Through our acts of obedience to his teachings
and commands, our faith becomes evident. Our obedience is
a response to God's love, a testament to our trust in him, and
a reflection of our commitment to follow his path (John 14:15;
Rom. 1:5; Heb. 11:8). Through obedience based in faith, we
not only affirm our belief but also participate in the unveiling
of God's will in our lives and in the world around us.

Embracing these truths invites us into a deeper, more authentic
relationship with God. Our faith not only believes but also acts. This
is the heart of abiding: it means living each day in the fullness of
faith, walking hand in hand with God, and aligning our steps with his
divine purpose.

My intention here is to capture the essence of our spiritual union
with the triune God through Christ in terms that resonate more deeply
and personally, moving beyond the technical connotations that the
word *alignment* might inadvertently convey.

Our relationship with the Father's will is not about the rigid
mechanics of alignment. It is about moving in step with the divine
rhythm, not in perfect precision or according to a fixed choreography
but in grace, fluidity, and responsiveness to God's lead by the Spirit.
It means moving in a relationship of mutual love, respect, and a deep
sense of connection.

As we learn to listen and respond to God's guidance, he transforms our steps into expressions of our love and trust in him. This
beautiful interaction with God softens the edges of our independence,
drawing us into a shared experience, enriching our spiritual lives, and
bringing us closer to the heart of the divine.

Abiding in the Vine

Bridging the stories of Saul and Truman with the spiritual practice of abiding in Jesus can offer insight into the essence of authentic spiritual life. For the follower of Jesus, there is no being authentically "spiritual" without the indwelling presence of the Holy Spirit.

Saul's tragic story points to the peril of navigating one's spiritual journey without being anchored in God's steadfast love and guidance by the Spirit. Truman's quest for authenticity and his courageous step beyond the confines of Seahaven symbolize the awakening to a life defined by truth and genuine relationship but falls short of the awakening that occurs when one is indwelt by the Spirit and chooses to abide in Jesus.

Abiding in the vine as Jesus describes in John 15:15 is not only a metaphor but also a call to life-transforming communion with him. Just as a vine provides nourishment and life to its branches, Jesus offers us the indwelling Spirit as the sustaining and regenerative source of spiritual sustenance and growth. Abiding in him implies a continuous, conscious choice to remain engaged with Christ's indwelling Spirit as our very life. In abiding, we draw on his strength, wisdom, and love to navigate the contours of life. Saul's life demonstrates the consequences of living disconnected from the Spirit. His reliance on his own understanding and strength led to spiritual blindness and a debilitating sense of alienation from Yahweh. Saul's life is a stark reminder of the void that forms when we choose to distance ourselves from the God of Abraham, Isaac, and Jacob.

Truman's journey is a powerful metaphor for the hunger and thirst necessary for spiritual awakening to occur. Truman's eventual escape from Seahaven can be seen symbolically to illustrate the liberation and fullness of life that comes when we venture out in the Spirit and pursue the God of truth. Abiding in Jesus by the Spirit invites the authentic life of union with God that continually relies on the divine presence.

Jesus beckons us with "Follow Me," summoning us to live our lives with an open-hearted embrace of his self-sacrificial, self-emptying love that guides, nurtures, and transforms us. To abide in Jesus is essentially to choose a path leading away from Saul's spiritual desolation and toward a more authentic, truth-filled life symbolized by Truman's breakthrough.

In abiding, our self-interest and the fleeting allure of sin no longer lead us. Instead, our desire to please God the Father (necessarily by faith) directs us in submitting to him—not as a loss of freedom but the discovery of real liberty in our divine design as image-bearers. This abiding is a practice that integrates mind, heart, and will in relationship with the One who calls us out of our ignorance and into the light of his truth. It is the practice of remaining in his presence, drawing sustenance from him, and allowing his life to flow through us.

This abiding is both a gift of grace and a disciplined pursuit. It requires our active participation and utter reliance on the triune God. As we abide in Christ, we become conduits of his life and love, bearing fruit that testifies to the transformative power of living in union with him. This way of living demands a countercultural stance that resists the seductions of a superficial age and embraces the slow, often hidden work of spiritual growth. It challenges us to prioritize the eternal over the temporal, the spiritual over the material, and the communal over the individualistic. In doing so, we not only experience personal transformation but also contribute to the cultivation of a community that reflects the triune God's beauty, holiness, and love.

In essence, the practice of abiding in Christ is the practice of resurrection life—a life that, though marked by the death of the old self, is characterized by the vibrancy, vitality, and fruitfulness of the new life in Christ. This is the heart of genuine spiritual formation: a life continually surrendered to and transformed by the triune God, bearing witness to the power of his grace and the reality of his kingdom in the here and now.

Practicing Resurrection

- Keeping the Truman character in mind, how does your life epitomize the ordinary? How does Truman's initial ignorance of his situation mirror unexamined areas of your life? How might these areas reflect unchallenged beliefs that hold sway in your life, consciously or unconsciously?

- Consider any effects in your life of information overload, polarizing narratives, success orientation, and the search for validation. How might they contribute to spiritual and psychological slumber and ways of living on autopilot? In what practical ways might you move toward consciousness and intentional living amid the noise?

- The human is prone to resisting, delaying, and outright defying God's direction, even for people indwelt by the Holy Spirit. How have you found yourself procrastinating in response to God's call? In what specific ways have you been reluctant to surrender certain personal desires or comforts that God seems to be highlighting? Can you address any specific areas of sluggishness in your spiritual disciplines and any impact to the practice of resurrection?

Notes

1. *The Truman Show*, directed by Peter Weir (Los Angeles: Paramount Pictures, 1998).
2. Erin Sullivan, "Self-Actualization," *Britannica*, accessed February 20, 2024, https://www.britannica.com/science/self-actualization.

5

Engaging the Healing Process

The praxis of abiding in Christ holds the potential for continual participation of God's triune life and provides an intimate way of knowing from the inside out. All of this is possible by way of the Spirit. As an experiential mode of knowing, it goes beyond acquiring information or grasping the surface of things. Instead, it involves a committed engagement with the Spirit that transforms our entire being.

In the light of Saul's narrative, we are reminded of the perils of unchecked fears, insecurities, and destructive rage that can derail our destinies. Yet the invitation to abide in Christ offers us a path of healing and restoration, a journey toward wholeness in the presence of the One who searches our hearts and tests our minds. The practice of abiding in Christ invites us to live in the constant flow of God's grace, where our hearts become the fertile ground for the Spirit's transformative work. It is here, in the sacred space of our interior temple, that we encounter the divine Surgeon who is ready to excise the thieves and robbers of our peace. By surrendering to this divine operation, we allow God to address the root causes of our fears and insecurities, not through a superficial overhaul but through a gentle, thorough cleansing of our wounds.

This healing process is foundational to acquiring a deeper way of knowing that transcends intellectual understanding and touches the core of our being. It shifts our perception, enabling us to discern not just the letter of the law but the heartbeat of the divine. This spiritual insight illuminates our path, guiding our decisions and actions from a place of healed vision and renewed purpose.

Moreover, abiding in Christ and allowing his Spirit to heal and renew us equips us to engage with the world around us in ways that reflect God's love and wisdom. It empowers us to confront challenges and make choices that flow from his self-sacrificial posture, fostering a life that is not only directed by the Spirit but also imbued with the Spirit's fruits: love, joy, peace, patience, kindness, goodness, faithfulness, gentleness, and self-control. As we continue to dwell in Christ, our relationship with the Spirit deepens, and we begin to understand John 14:26, which promises that the Holy Spirit will teach us all things and remind us of everything Jesus has said. This promise of the Spirit's guidance is the cornerstone of our journey toward a deeper knowing. It assures us that we are not left to navigate life's complexities alone but are accompanied and led by the Spirit of Truth who reveals God's wisdom and direction from the inside out.

The Ways of Understanding: A Holistic Approach

In 1 Corinthians 2, Paul articulates the essence of spiritual discernment, emphasizing that the wisdom we speak among the mature is fundamentally different from the wisdom of this age. That maturity is the result of a way of knowing that is cruciform (2:6–7).

Michael Gorman plainly says, "The distinctive feature of Paul's experience of the Spirit, and his resulting understanding of the essence of this Spirit, is the paradoxical symbiosis (union) of power and weakness, of power and cruciformity."[1] This concept of being shaped by the cross of Christ deepens the paradox Gorman describes. For Paul, the cross is not only a historical event; it is a paradigm through which our lives are to be understood and lived. The cross represents the ultimate expression of God's power through weakness—Christ's victorious defeat of sin and death through his own suffering and death. Thus, knowing through the Spirit involves embracing the cruciform pattern as the way God operates in the world and in our lives as believers.

The symbiotic relationship between power and weakness challenges and enriches our way of knowing in at least four coupled ways:

- *Humility and dependence:* By recognizing that true power comes through our reliance on God, we cultivate humility and a deep dependence on the Spirit. This posture shifts our source of confidence from self to God, fostering a trust in divine strength that transcends human limitations.

- *Empathy and compassion:* Understanding that God's power is revealed in weakness opens us up to a deeper empathy and compassion for the suffering and vulnerabilities of others. It attunes our hearts to God's heart, which is moved by the plight of the broken and the marginalized.

- *Resilience and hope:* Embracing weakness as the locus of divine power instills a resilient hope in the face of trials and tribulations. It assures us that God is at work even in the midst of suffering, transforming what the world sees as weakness into channels of his grace and power.

- *Mission and witness:* This paradoxical way of knowing shapes our mission and witness in the world. It compels a witness to Christ that is characterized by self-giving, self-sacrificial love, service, and the proclamation of a gospel that triumphs through sacrifice, mirroring the pattern of the cross.

Paul's experiential knowledge of the Spirit, marked by the intertwining of power and weakness, offers a profound way of knowing that redefines our understanding of strength, success, and influence. It invites us to partake of what he refers to in 1 Corinthians 1:9 as "the fellowship of the Son" in a way that is deeply countercultural (ESV). Through this fellowship, our weakness becomes a conduit of the Spirit's power. This is the embodying of the paradoxical power of the cross in our lives that results from experientially knowing and following Christ. It is a way of knowing by the Spirit that is not merely cognitive but existential, shaping how we live, love, and serve in a world that tends to value power that is devoid of vulnerability.

The distinction between "fellowship *of* the Son" and "fellowship *with* the Son" seems subtle but carries theological and linguistic implications that significantly influence our understanding of communion and identity with the triune God. In the English language, *of* and *with* serve different functions. Linguistically, *of* often denotes possession or origin, implying belonging or emanation from a source. However, *with* indicates accompaniment or association, suggesting a relationship between separate entities.

In addition, "the fellowship of the Son" suggests a greater level of participation in the life and being of Christ. It conveys a sense of belonging to the very essence and communion of the Son, with the Father and by the Spirit. This implies a fellowship that is not just alongside him; it is a shared participation in the triune life because we partake by his Spirit in his divine nature (2 Pet. 1:4). Understanding the "fellowship *of* the Son" reveals a transformative union with Christ that redefines our identity. This mystical union, central to Paul's teachings, means we live *in Christ* and he lives *in us* (see Gal. 2:20). This suggests a merging of our lives with his. This connection reshapes our sense of self, not as solitary followers but as integral members of Christ's body, intimately sharing in his life, suffering, death, and resurrection.

This concept extends beyond a personal connection with Jesus, drawing us into the wider Christian community, where we collectively participate in the divine life. Choosing *of* over *with* enriches our understanding of the church's sacramental and liturgical life. More than worshiping in Christ's presence, we are actively participating in the life he shares with the Father and the Spirit. From this perspective, the Eucharist transitions from being a memorial meal to being a means of participating in the Son's body and blood.

Thus, the phrase "fellowship of the Son" profoundly affects our theological insights, spiritual identity, and community life. It encourages us to see our relationship with Christ not just as companionship but as participation in his divine essence, facilitated by the Holy Spirit. This deeper engagement urges us toward a more meaningful interaction with the transformative and communal facets of our faith. By embracing the fellowship of the Son, we enter a relational and participatory way of knowing that is anchored in the shared divine communion of the Father, Son, and Holy Spirit. This knowledge is holistic, involving not just the mind but the entire being—heart, soul, mind, and strength—and immersing us in God's presence. There, our identity is forged in our unity with Christ, making us beloved children of God and co-heirs with Christ.

This participatory understanding of faith enables us to live out the mysteries of our belief from within. Our grasp of God's kingdom and will is deepened by our active participation in Christ's life, guided by the Spirit into all truth. We are reshaped into Christ's image, personally and as a community, enriching our insights into love, justice, mercy, and truth, not merely through thought but through our lived experience.

Furthermore, the fellowship of the Son fosters a communal dimension of knowing. In the church's community, wisdom is not only acquired but shared and discerned together. This emphasizes that our faith is a collective journey, enriched by our mutual interactions, service, and love. This fellowship also encompasses a sacramental way of knowing in which our encounters with Christ transcend language and touch our essence. These tangible, grace-filled experiences of Christ's life meld the spiritual with the physical while unveiling the sacramental nature of creation. In essence, the fellowship of the Son beckons us into a dynamic, relational, and transformative way of knowing that is deeply personal and transformative.

Importance in the Current Context

The fellowship *of* the Son is important in our current context for several reasons:

- *It contrasts sharply with the posture that Saul adopted regarding his kingship.* In a world increasingly fragmented by individualism, polarization, and disconnection, the fellowship of the Son calls us back to our foundational identity in Christ, emphasizing unity, communal responsibility, and a shared life in the Spirit. This is diametrically opposite to Saul's approach, which was characterized by isolation, disobedience, and a reliance on his own strength and understanding.

- *It is a remedy for isolation.* In an era when loneliness and isolation are rampant, the fellowship of the Son reminds us that we are not alone. Our identity and purpose are found in being part of Christ's body and knitted together with other believers. This communal aspect is vital for mental, emotional, and spiritual health, offering a sense of belonging and shared purpose.

- *It is an antidote to polarization.* In an era rife with division, this fellowship encourages unity in diversity. It calls for a posture of humility, mutual respect, and love that transcends differences, modeling a way of being that our societies desperately need.

- *It is countercultural to individualism.* The modern emphasis on individual achievement and autonomy often leads to a self-centered approach to life. However, the fellowship of the Son invites us into a relational, participatory life that orients our actions beyond personal success, toward the well-being of the community and the glory of God.

Contrast with Saul's Posture

Saul based his kingship not on God's commands but on reliance on his own judgment. This approach led to disobedience and Saul's eventual downfall. The fellowship of the Son is grounded in a deep dependence on God, recognizing that true strength and wisdom come from surrendering to his will. Saul often acted unilaterally, making decisions that benefited his reign but harmed his relationship with God and his people. The fellowship of the Son emphasizes interdependence and shared responsibility. These help us to nurture and edify one another, highlighting a leadership model that is servant oriented rather than power centered.

Saul's refusal to submit to God's will and his inability to confront his own shortcomings led to spiritual stagnation. Conversely, the fellowship of the Son is inherently transformational, constantly inviting us into growth, healing, and renewal by the Spirit. It is a dynamic process of becoming more like Christ, individually and collectively.

At this juncture in history, the fellowship of the Son presents a radically different and much-needed posture toward life, ways of knowing, and ways of leading. It calls for a return to our core identity as beloved children of God, living in intimate relationship with him and in authentic community with each other. This way of being not only remedies many modern societal and personal ailments but also serves as a powerful witness to the world of the transformative power of the gospel.

Saul did not fathom the repercussions of his choices but became enmeshed in fear, pride, and isolation. We can easily make the same mistake but are invited into the safety of humility, service, and dependence on God. Knowing by the Spirit involves a direct (1 Cor. 2:6–13), heart-and-soul encounter with the God of Abraham, Isaac, and Jacob. By definition, this exceeds an intellectual grasp. The Spirit's presence within us enhances our personal and communal relationships with the triune God. This helps us to discern our paths and face life's challenges, not purely with intellectual acumen but with the divine insight Paul highlighted in the concept of "the fellowship of the Son" (1:9 ESV).

Scriptural Insight and Historical Parallel

In contemporary society and culture, we stand in a liminal space—a threshold at which the past and future overlap and the lessons of history meet the possibilities of tomorrow. This space, filled with uncertainty and potential, demands that we truly grasp the significance of multiple times.

If we were to identify current aspects of liminal space, we would admit that issues such as artificial intelligence, globalization, environmental concerns, climate change, sociopolitical polarization, cultural shifts, and cyberwarfare present major challenges and high levels of uncertainty. The impact of these matters on the personal and collective psyche cannot be ignored.

The ancient Israelite sages discerned the nuances of their era and understood the needs of their times. We are similarly called. In the gap between what was and what is, we necessarily face our future and the opportunity to shape it. In some ways but not all, the wisdom of the past will inform our approach. Our epoch, like many before it, is one of crisis that could lead to transformation. In this overlapping of times, we need insights and guidance to move us forward with purpose and hope.

T. S. Eliot drew inspiration from the priest, Saint John of the Cross, weaving his mystical concepts into the fabric of "East Coker," Eliot's second of four quartets. The poem explores themes of time, human experience, and the search for meaning, echoing Saint John's call for renunciation in the pursuit of deeper truths. Much as Saint John's ascent to Mount Carmel symbolizes the soul's journey toward union with God, Eliot's poem reflects the cyclical nature of life, the inevitability of death, and the possibility of rebirth through spiritual surrender, as this excerpt shows:

> To arrive where you are, to get from where you are not,
> You must go by a way wherein there is no ecstasy.
> In order to arrive at what you do not know
> You must go by a way which is the way of ignorance.
> In order to possess what you do not possess
> You must go by the way of dispossession.
> In order to arrive at what you are not
> You must go through the way in which you are not.
> And what you do not know is the only thing you know
> And what you own is what you do not own
> And where you are is where you are not.[2]

The idea of arriving at where you are implies that understanding and accepting who you are means experiencing and exploring whom you are not. It's about the journey of self-discovery that often involves exploring unfamiliar or uncomfortable paths. When Eliot tells us there is "no ecstasy" in the path, he suggests that the journey to self-understanding is not always joyful or enlivened by ecstatic revelations.

Its experiences are often mundane, difficult, and even painful yet crucial for growth.

Eliot notes that to discover new knowledge or truths, we must first acknowledge our ignorance. The journey he describes involves the humility of not knowing yet remaining open to learning and new experiences. He moves us to the paradox of possession through dispossession. Therefore, to truly possess or understand something (such as a deeper sense of self or some other profound truth), we might need to let go of certain possessions or preconceptions. This is about the freedom and insight gained when we release our hold on material or fixed ideas.

Equally intriguing is the notion of arriving at whom we are not. Eliot invites us to understand our true selves by exploring and acknowledging aspects of ourselves with which we might not identify at first. Through contrast and difference, then, there is growth, all of it leading us to embrace the unknown.

If Eliot's proposition is correct, the only thing we truly know is that *we don't know what we don't know*. Thus, he beckons us to value the embrace of uncertainty and see the unknown as as a font of true knowledge and self. In essence, there is a paradox of ownership and presence together. What you and I own in terms of knowledge or understanding is often that which we have not yet grasped fully. Similarly, where you and I are is often where we feel we are not, suggesting that personal growth involves being in states of transition and uncertainty.

In *The Ascent of Mount Carmel*, Saint John of the Cross lays down a series of paradoxical injunctions aimed at guiding the soul toward the summit of spiritual union, the high estate of Mount Carmel:

1. That thou mayest have pleasure in everything, seek pleasure in nothing.
2. That thou mayest know everything, seek to know nothing.

3. That thou mayest possess all things, seek to possess nothing.

4. That thou mayest be everything, seek to be nothing.

5. That thou mayest attain to that in which thou hast no pleasure, thou must walk there where thou hast no pleasure.

6. That thou mayest attain to that which thou knowest not, thou must go through that which thou knowest not.

7. That thou mayest attain to that which thou possessest not, thou must go through that which thou possessest not.

8. That thou mayest attain to that which thou art not, thou must go through that which thou art not.[3]

These deeply spiritual and interior instructions propose a path of negation as the means to ultimate fulfillment and union with the divine. Saint John advocates for a detachment from all things—pleasure, knowledge, possessions, and even one's own sense of self—to attain the fullness of spiritual union.

In comparing Saint John of the Cross and T. S. Eliot, we find a shared understanding of the paradox at the heart of our spiritual and existential quests. Both men suggest that true fulfillment and understanding come not through the accumulation of experiences, knowledge, or possessions but through their relinquishment. Saint John's instructions for ascending to spiritual union emphasize the necessity of emptying oneself of desires and attachments to encounter the divine directly. Similarly, Eliot's poetry suggests that wisdom and enlightenment are not found in clinging to what is tangible and known but in embracing the mystery and uncertainty of existence.

Three Voices and the Practice of Resurrection

In the context of our current liminality, the practice of resurrection (the transformative journey of renewal and rebirth) finds resonance in the spiritual paths illuminated by Saint Paul, T. S. Eliot, and Saint

John of the Cross. Saint Paul's insights into knowing by the Spirit, as articulated in 1 Corinthians 2, invite us into a new way of understanding that transcends human wisdom through the fellowship of the Son. This divine way of knowing, much like the contemplative journeys described by Saint John of the Cross and the poetic reflections of T. S. Eliot, calls for a path of negation—a letting go of worldly attachments, ego, and the superficial layers that obscure our true essence.

In a society marked by rapid transitions and overwhelming complexity, this spiritual orientation offers a compelling alternative to the relentless pursuit of material success and self-gratification. It beckons us toward a more meaningful existence, grounded in the Spirit's transformative power. Just as Eliot and Saint John of the Cross articulate a journey through darkness as a pathway to light, so too does the practice of resurrection embody this movement from death to life, inviting us to embrace our vulnerabilities and surrender our pretenses in order to encounter the profound depths of God's wisdom and love.

By integrating Saint Paul's teaching on the Spirit's indwelling with the mystical insights of Saint John of the Cross and Eliot's poetic wisdom, we are guided to the mysterious place of unknowing. This is a place of spiritual convergence where true knowledge and transformation can occur—a space in which we embrace our limitations and the unknown as fertile ground for divine encounter and rebirth. It offers us a way forward that is both ancient and acutely relevant for our times.

The practice of resurrection challenges us as individuals and communities to embrace vulnerability and transformation. This is akin to the biblical concept of dying to oneself in order to find life in Christ (John 12:24–25). It encourages the collective reevaluation of values, priorities, and the essence of what it means to live fully and authentically. Amid our digital connections, environmental crises, and social fragmentation, the practice of resurrection becomes a radical act of hope, renewal, and wholeness in a fractured world.

This journey of transformation, inspired by Saint Paul's insights into knowing by the Spirit, propels us through the internal landscape of faith and understanding, often without the need for full articulation. It invites us into a seamless engagement with the spiritual principles that underpin the practice of resurrection, allowing us to internalize divine truths in ways that go beyond simple explanation. This spiritual path fosters an intuitive grasp of silent yet profound divine realities able to enrich our personal and communal transformation with experiential wisdom that guides the soul through the nuances of growth and renewal.

This spiritual odyssey bears witness to our innate capacity for growth, transformation, and deeper understanding. It underscores that true fulfillment emerges not from the accumulation of material possessions or accolades but from the profound simplicity of seeking and embodying the divine presence. Here, negation becomes a form of affirmation, and what appears as reversal becomes the new order—a testament to the transformative power of embracing the Spirit's leading.

This approach is more than a pathway to personal enlightenment; it is a blueprint for continuous renewal and is marked by a longing to engage with the world through love, purpose, and wonder. The practice of resurrection, as illuminated by these spiritual insights, invites us to a life where every ending is a beginning and every loss is steeped in the promise of new life and deeper communion with the divine. It's a journey that affirms our participation in the fellowship of the Son, where knowing by the Spirit becomes the bedrock of our faith and the lens through which we view our existence and calling.

──────────── **Practicing Resurrection** ────────────

- Abiding in Christ empowers us to confront challenges and make choices that flow from his self-sacrificial posture. How does this posture change your approach to life's everyday difficulties, disruptions, and seeming missteps? How has a life that is not only directed by the Spirit but also imbued with the Spirit's fruits (love, joy, peace, patience, kindness, goodness, faithfulness, gentleness, and self-control) turned moments of challenge into opportunities for change and renewal?

- How does the "fellowship of the Son" alter your position as someone who is traveling *alongside* Christ and instead impart a sense of sharing and participation in the triune life by the Spirit? Be specific in relation to how this distinction changes your viewpoint going forward.

- Consider the text of T. S. Eliot's "East Coker." Which words or lines speak most directly to your current sense of self and place? How do they capture your own thoughts and feelings? How do they express what previously seemed inexpressible?

Notes

1. Michael J. Gorman, *Cruciformity: Paul's Narrative Spirituality of the Cross* (Grand Rapids, MI: Eerdmans, 2001), 52.
2. T. S. Eliot, "East Coker," in *The Four Quartets* (San Diego: Harcourt Brace, 1988).
3. Saint John of the Cross, *The Ascent of Mount Carmel*, ed. Benedict Zimmermann, trans. David Lewis (London: Thomas Baker, 1906), 58–59.

6

Embracing Your Shadow Self

In an era marked by chaos and uncertainty, the quest for personal and communal healing draws us to narratives that transcend time and culture. Continuing the juxtaposition of ancient Scripture and modern mythology, let's consider the contrasting journeys of King Saul and Peter Parker (particularly as he is depicted in the Marvel Cinematic Universe's *Spider-Man* films). Through their stories, we find ourselves confronting the shadow self—a concept that is deeply rooted in Jungian psychology—and the transformative potential within this struggle. The aim is to illuminate the path toward wholeness, drawing from the rich tapestry of biblical narrative, the hero's journey, and the archetype of the modern superhero.

The Shadow: A Jungian Perspective

For Jung, the *shadow* is comprised of the repressed and suppressed aspects of ourselves that we deem unacceptable and prefer to disown.

However, "the shadow is a living part of the personality and therefore wants to live with it [the personality] in some form. It cannot be argued out of existence or rationalized into harmlessness."[1] The shadow is a fundamental aspect of being human; it is entwined with our capacity for good, as it contains potential energies and qualities that, when acknowledged and integrated, can enrich our lives. The concept of the shadow is one of the most profound and enduring contributions to Jung's understanding of the human psyche.

In Jung's quoted statement, to "live with it" means to live with the personality at large. The shadow desires not only to recognized but to be integrated within the self. The goal is for the shadow's collection of repressed, ignored, or undeveloped aspects of our identity to coexist and be harmonized within the conscious life, suggesting that integration is not just beneficial but essential for psychological health and wholeness.

The assertion that the shadow "cannot be argued out of existence" emphasizes the futility of denial in dealing with our deeper, often darker, aspects. The shadow's persistence lies in its connection in the unconscious; it remains a part of us regardless of our attempts to ignore or negate its existence through logic. This speaks to the shadow's resilience and the need to confront and understand these aspects of ourselves in the journey toward self-awareness and individuation.

The idea that the shadow cannot be "rationalized into harmlessness" addresses our tendency to minimize or justify the shadow's influence through intellectualization. Therefore, Jung's theory cautions against the oversimplification of the shadow's complexities and potential dangers. Rationalizing the shadow's presence or effects does not neutralize its power; instead, it often bypasses the crucial work of engaging with and transforming these aspects in a meaningful way. Integration involves acknowledging the shadow's full impact and learning to work with its energies constructively rather than attempting to dilute or dismiss them. For Jung, embracing the full spectrum of our being, including the shadow, is a pathway to individuation—the process of becoming one's true self.

This journey entails honest self-reflection, acceptance of our complexities, and the courage to transform the raw materials of our psyche into a more unified and authentic whole. By acknowledging that the shadow "wants to live with [the personality] in some form," we open ourselves to the possibility of a richer, more integrated existence, in which the shadow becomes a vital companion in our personal and spiritual development rather than an adversary to be defeated.

The question is, how can we better grasp acknowledging the shadow and therefore open ourselves to a richer and more integrated existence?

Peter Parker: A Modern Hero's Confrontation with the Shadow

In the heart of New York City, Peter Parker emerges as the quintessential young hero. Thrust into a world where extraordinary powers imply immense responsibility, Peter navigates the complexities of his new abilities and the trials of adolescence with a depth of character that sets him apart from many more traditional heroes. Unlike King Saul, whose inability to confront his inner shadows led to jealousy, fear, and downfall, Peter embodies the journey of self-reflection, growth, and humility. His battles, notably against the Vulture and Mysterio, transcend physical confrontations, reflecting deeper struggles with guilt, grief, and the temptation to shirk responsibility. These adversaries, exploiting Peter's vulnerabilities, serve as mirrors to his deepest fears and insecurities, challenging his moral compass and perception of reality.

However, it is Peter's unwavering adherence to the principle that "with great power comes great responsibility" that truly distinguishes his narrative. This commitment drives his journey not only toward heroism but transforming personal growth, echoing the timeless themes of duty, desire, strength, and vulnerability that define the hero's journey. Peter's story resonates as a modern mythos, paralleling ancient tales of transformation and redemption. His response to adversity, characterized by moments of self-reflection and repentance, underscores a deepening understanding of service and heroism.

Peter Parker's resilience is formed by his duty to his community and willingness to embrace his shortcomings. Spider-Man's journey holds up a mirror to ours and reminds us that responsibility comes with physical, political, and personal power. He navigates his failings with an open heart and illuminates the path toward becoming the truest version of himself, marked by integrity and purpose amid life's overwhelming challenges.

Parker's story typifies our potential to emerge from our trials stronger, having learned and grown through our fears, failures, internal struggles, and external battles. His dramatic transformation as an ordinary high school student catapulted into the realm of the extraordinary resonates deep with us. Imbued with newfound powers, Peter enters the whirlwind of responsibility and moral quandaries that epitomize the hero's journey. Peter experiences his odyssey in a delicate and paradoxical balance between his mundane existence and the colossal weight of being Spider-Man.

Integral to Peter's evolution is the lesson he learns through heart-rending losses. His Uncle Ben and mentor, Tony Stark, have served not only as Peter's guardians but as beacons guiding him through the tumult of youth and heroism. In losing them, he discovers the value of sacrifice and necessity of carving his own path. As he emerges from their shadows and into his own life, he embraces his unique calling with courage and humility.

I appreciate the Spider-Man narrative as an adult, but my connection to the character began in my childhood. One of my cherished possessions was my collection of Spider-Man comics, beginning in August of 1962 and including the *Spider-Man Number 1 Annual*, featuring the Sinister Six. This comic and the rest of my pristine collection became lost treasures of my youth when, unbeknown to me, my mother discarded them in a decluttering campaign. The words of the late comedian Jonathan Winters ring true: "Oh the pain, the pain!" (And yes, from a Jungian perspective, I needed inner healing from my "mother complex"!)

On a more serious tone, Spider-Man's journey evolved amid my childhood memories of real-life calamities like the Cuban missile crisis. Spider-Man found a place in my consciousness in the days of public school bomb, the space race, the Vietnam War, and the civil rights movement. Characters like him captured my imagination because they were "just like us." Yet in their ordinariness, they learned to take on daunting and even mortal enemies.

Given the nuanced, twenty-first-century challenges of technology, artificial intelligence, identity, and social responsibility, "Spidey's" numerous iterations have matched the accelerating speed of change. As he reflects our shifting societal landscape, however, the core of his appeal remains unchanged. The character continues to inspire, embodying the timeless struggle of the human condition through his perseverance, resilience, and unwavering commitment to justice. Whether in comic books, movies, animated series, or video games, he invites each generation to find elements of their own life in Peter Parker's journey. And he reminds us that we, too, can rise above our challenges and embrace our destinies with grace and valor.

Saul's Descent: A Tale of Unconfronted Shadows

Saul's story has a decidedly unhappy ending. When I was a child, such endings unsettled me. Truth be told, they still do. They ignite a desire to alter outcomes, mend what has been broken, and redeem the characters who fell short of my hopes. My reaction is not unique but human. As adults we know that life does not always grant us fairy-tale endings. This realization prompts a search for answers that transcend the visible world and point us toward deeper truths.

The momentous disorientation resulting from humanity's presumption to discern "good and evil" without divine wisdom has left us with lasting wounds, vulnerabilities, and feelings of alienation and isolation. This fractured state creates spaces within us where darkness can dwell, obscured in the shadows of our hearts and minds—and it is this fact that makes Saul's story so poignant for me.

As I read his narrative, I long for redemption and a different ending. This yearning points us all to the ultimate resolution found in the One who entered our condition to invite us into his. In Christ, all hopes for transformation and for becoming who we were meant to be find their fulfillment. Through this lens, Saul's story expands beyond a tale of what was lost and discloses the way toward the "more" that is offered in the person of Jesus Christ.

So much of Saul's pain emanated from the issues that lay buried in the depths of his unconscious mind, only to haunt him later. This is an easy experience for us to understand. If the twenty-first century has taught us anything, it has apprised us of the ways that reality breaks into the present and resurrects the pains of the past. Often, it happens through "wild card" events—the unforeseeable, high-impact occurrences that dramatically alter the course of our personal and collective trajectories.

Although grappling with plausible, possible, and preferable futures is challenging all by itself, these wild cards (which Nassim Nicholas Taleb rebranded as "black swans" in 2007)[2] introduce a new dimension of unpredictability. They significantly intensify our inclination toward closure in situations where closure is nonexistent. This in turn prompts us to suppress, repress, or bury unresolved issues within the shadowy recesses of our psyche, much as Saul had done. This insistence on finding resolution mirrors a deeper psychological struggle. As Carl Jung observed, "We cannot change anything unless we accept it. Condemnation does not liberate, it oppresses."[3]

Jung's statement notes a crucial aspect of human nature: we prefer to avoid confronting life's uncomfortable or painful realities. Shock and disorientation tempt us to retreat into the caverns of our interiority in hopes of shielding ourselves from the perceived perils of the unknown. The disruptive and disturbing effects of black swan events can make these self-protective tendencies even more pronounced.

Instead of affording us the protection we seek, our retreat obscures those parts of ourselves that require acknowledgment and integration for true healing and growth to occur. The challenge, then, is not only to anticipate or respond to wild card events but to courageously confront the unresolved aspects of our inner world. Then we can begin to navigate life's unpredictable waters with resilience, openness, and a deeper understanding of our own capacity to adapt and be transformed.

In this regard, Saul's story serves as a cautionary tale—not only a tragic reminder of how our unresolved internal conflicts can foretell a downfall but an invitation to learn from his unfinished business and our own choices. Saul's story is sprinkled with moments that, if interpreted correctly, could have placed him on the journey of a fully consummated hero. By more consciously interacting with his fears and shortcomings, he could have moved from fragmentation to integration, and from brokenness to wholeness.

The pivotal and often intimidating moments in our lives are laden with potential for transformation. They beckon us to discern the signs in our own lives that might guide us toward healing and fulfillment. For Saul, his encounter with Samuel the seer and prophet was an inflection point. Their ensuing relationship exposed him to a world freighted with unseen mystery and the presence of the Sovereign God of Israel. His anointment as king and even his moments of profound fear and doubt were opportunities for self-reflection and reorientation toward a more integrated self. Instead of retreating into his shadows, Saul could have embraced these signs and allowed them to illuminate his inner shadows. This would have freed him to seek guidance beyond his immediate understanding and trust in a narrative larger than his ego's fears and ambitions.

Saul's choice to retreat is a familiar and forgivable one. All of us have made Saul's choice in one way or another and forfeited the self-discovery and redemption that present themselves along the hero's journey. Saul's story is simply a road map marking the roads not taken, in his life and ours. It pinpoints our own internal wildernesses on the way to wholeness and integration. Although his story is already written, it finds redemption in numerous ways. Here we see that it warns us to choose a different path. It prods us to engage with the shadowy areas in the depths of our being. And it reminds us that we are not beyond the reach of divine grace.

It is true that Saul's potential for greatness was over-shadowed (pun intended) by his inability to face his insecurities and his growing paranoia, particularly regarding David. And yes, Saul's unconfronted fears, need for control, and resistance to divine guidance had tragic implications. He lacked the self-awareness that Peter Parker developed. Therefore, he was far less open to transformation. Whereas Peter Parker learned to accept help, forgive himself for his shortcomings, and dedicate himself anew to his Spider-Man role, Saul allowed the shadowy places to confine him. Instead of embodying Jung's concept of individuation, as Parker did, Saul remained incarcerated by shadows and did not enter the process of becoming whole. He unwittingly resisted the integration of the shadow and the alignment of his personal mission with God's higher purpose for his life.

The Hero's Journey

The heroic journey can be looked at from a perspective of analytical psychology,[4] or the monomyth, as conceptualized by Joseph Campbell,[5] which captures the essence of the hero's narrative across cultures and epochs. In addressing the issue of Campbell's influence on Jung and others, and on the hero's journey itself, Chris Vogler says emphatically, "the Hero's Journey is as important an emotional or psychological journey as it is physical."[6] This journey, marked by stages such as the call to adventure, the road of trials, the apotheosis, and the return, mirrors the universal quest for growth, discovery, and transformation.

Campbell's work unveils the hero within every story and, more importantly, within every individual, suggesting that each person's life follows a heroic narrative pattern, characterized by challenges, revelations, and periods of intense change. Carl Jung's exploration of individuation parallels Campbell's monomyth, providing a psychological framework for understanding the quest of becoming aware of oneself, integrating the unconscious with the conscious, and achieving a whole, unique identity. This individuation involves confronting and reconciling the shadow self—the unacknowledged, often undesirable aspects of one's personality—with one's persona, the public face shown to the world. This journey toward wholeness is akin to the hero's quest, requiring the individual to delve into the depths of their psyche, face their darkest fears, and emerge transformed.

Within this context, the narrative of the Incarnate Son, Jesus Christ, stands as the grand archetypal image of the quintessential hero. Christ's incarnation, ministry, death, and resurrection embody the ultimate hero's journey, encapsulating themes of sacrifice, redemption, and victory over death. Unlike the heroes of myth who seek glory, treasure, or personal enlightenment, Christ's journey is one of self-emptying love and obedience to the divine will, offering a new

paradigm for heroism. His path illuminates the way for all who seek
to follow him, inviting believers to embark on their own heroic quests,
not for self-aggrandizement but for the sake of love, service, and the
transformation of the world.

The interplay between the monomyth, Jung's individuation, and
the life of Christ offers a rich tapestry for understanding the contours
of our spiritual and psychological journeys. Through the lens of these
narratives, we can discern the movements of grace in our lives, guiding us through our trials and tribulations toward a deeper communion with the divine. As we navigate our personal heroic journeys,
informed by the wisdom of Campbell and Jung and inspired by the
example of Christ, we are invited into a process of continual growth,
self-discovery, and the embrace of our calling to live out the virtues of
the kingdom of God in a broken world.

Through a Jungian lens we could speak of Saul failing to confront his shadow self. Jung's own words explain the value of such a
confrontation:

> This confrontation is the first test of courage on the inner way, a
> test sufficient to frighten off most people, for the meeting with our-
> selves belongs to the more unpleasant things that can be avoided so
> long as we can project everything negative into the environment.
> But if we are able to see our own shadow and can bear knowing
> about it, then a small part of the problem has already been solved:
> we have at least brought up the personal unconscious.[7]

Embarking on a journey to understand ourselves—including our
shadows, fears, and struggles—is a path not everyone is prepared
to tread. Jung admits that courage is required to confront the parts
of ourselves we're not proud of. He marks it as the first step toward
discovering our true selves. Yet it's within our faith that this journey
transforms from merely bearable to one brimming with hope. Jesus

and the Holy Spirit aren't just companions on this adventure; they are our guides, illuminating the path with the light of divine love and wisdom.

Jesus is not confined to the pages of history. As professed in the faith once delivered to the saints, he is the "radiance of God's glory and the exact representation of His being" (Heb. 1:3 NIV). The Nicene Creed echoes this truth, declaring Jesus as "God from God, Light from Light, True God from True God, Begotten not made, of the same essence as the Father."[8] Yet this divine radiance chose to live among us as Mary's Boy, fully embracing the complexities of humanity yet without sin. Jesus of Nazareth, the God-Man, exemplifies the life we are called to lead—a life marked by self-sacrificial love and the courage to face our darkest moments as a path toward transformation. He navigated every challenge, not by avoidance but through obedience to the Father and surrender to the Spirit, demonstrating how grace operates from the inside out.

The Heroic Healing Journey

In facing our own struggles and the parts of ourselves we prefer to conceal, we are not alone. Jesus stands with us, not at a distance but intimately close, offering freedom and wholeness. Understanding this, we know that our journey of self-discovery is not a solitary one. It is a shared pilgrimage with Christ, whose presence illuminates even the deepest shadows. Jesus, embodying both divine radiance and human vulnerability, shows us that grace is not just a concept but a lived reality, transforming us from within and guiding us toward the fullness of life he promises.

Consider the Holy Spirit as the living presence of God within us, breathing life into our being and connecting us to the Trinity's divine dance. The Spirit whispers to our hearts, affirming our identity as beloved children of God, and inviting us to cry out with Jesus, "Abba! Father!" (Rom. 8:15). In moments of doubt or fear, when facing our depths is daunting, the Holy Spirit offers a gentle reassurance, saying, "You are not walking this path alone." The indwelling Spirit, our compassionate guide, encourages us to confront our fears and uncover our true selves. Not singularly focused on our missteps, the Spirit envelops us in the vastness of God's love and mercy so we can face our shadows, learn from our experiences, and embrace the growth that comes from facing our challenges in his presence.

Peter Parker's story reminds us through parallel, and Saul's story reminds us through contrast, that opening our hearts to the transformation is the way to healing. But that transformation comes from the triune God. Then we not only find out who we are; we discover who we can become in Christ. We realize that we can be fully loved, fully accepted, and fully alive.

We are not condemned to manifest the unchecked shadow self, as it was seen in Saul's kingship. We are not inherently unable to face our fears and insecurities. We are not doomed to exert aggression as a means of control. Nor was Saul doomed in these ways. The consequences of spiritual and psychological fragmentation seen in Cain can be avoided when we embrace self-awareness and divine guidance. Saul's odyssey drove him into the depths of his own inner abyss and ultimate death. Every hero's journey is, in essence, an inward voyage that can end as Saul's did or can lead to the integration of the self's myriad aspects.

Saul's narrative is not an opportunity to gloat. It is a journey into the heart of every honest and self-aware pastor and leader. I can attest to traveling the shadowy caves of my heart, and I continue to do so, confronting parts of myself that threaten to undermine my leadership. These travels challenge and often disconcert me, but they uncover potential that has been buried under layers of fear, anxiety, and the scars from relational struggles. These personal and observed experiences, amassed over fifty years of preaching the gospel and engaging with leaders and laypeople have exposed me to the full spectrum of human experience, including the highest highs and the deepest lows. Each story and exchange has humbled me, awakened me to my great need of God, and drawn me into the Jesus Prayer, which simply says, "Lord Jesus, Son of David, have mercy on me."

Turning a sober gaze toward Saul's story nudges us to look for signs that we are honestly seeking God. Saul's life was painful, having been marked by his failure to seek God's guidance. A long shadow revealed the inevitable emptiness that can pervade our lives when we attempt to face life in our own strength.

In the final analysis, the genuine hero's journey is enfolded in our lives with Christ, who is the Hero within.

Practicing Resurrection

- Thinking about King Saul and Peter Parker, what kind of relationship have you cultivated with your shadows? Have you compartmentalized them deep in your unconscious mind, as Saul did? Are recurring issues like jealousy, fear, insecurity, and others nagging you as a result? Or is your approach more like Peter's, embodying the journey of self-reflection, growth, and humility—and, therefore, healing? Explain with objectivity but also gentleness.

- Assuming that individuation involves confronting and reconciling the unacknowledged, often undesirable aspects (the shadows) of your personality with the face you show to the world, can you first identify the shadows? Once identified, consider what the price of concealing them has been over time. Conversely, what is the value of facing even your darkest fears?

- How can a more compassionate view toward Saul's (and other people's) greatest failings give you permission to accept your own shortfalls? Conversely, how might a harsh view toward his (and their) damaging choices forbid you to forgive yourself?

Notes

1. C. G. Jung, *Collected Works of C. G. Jung*, vol. 9, part 1, *Archetypes and the Collective Unconscious* (Princeton, NJ: Princeton University Press, 2014), 20, Kindle.
2. Nassim Nicholas Taleb, *The Black Swan: The Impact of the Highly Improbable*, 2nd ed. (New York: Random House, 2010).
3. Frith Luton, "The Heroic Journey—A Jungian Perspective," FrithLuton.com, accessed February 19, 2024, https://frithluton.com/articles/heroic-journey -jungian-perspective/.
4. Luton, "The Heroic Journey—A Jungian Perspective."
5. Joseph Campbell, *The Hero with a Thousand Faces*, 3rd ed. (Novato, CA: New World Library, 2008).
6. Christopher Vogler, foreword to *Myth and the Movies: Discovering the Mythic Structure of 50 Unforgettable Films*, by Stuart Voytilla (Studio City, CA: Michael Wiese Productions, 1999), page #.
7. Jung, *Archetypes and Collective Unconscious*, 20.
8. Scott Hoeze, "The Nicene Creed," Banner, January 18, 2011, https:// www.thebanner.org/features/2011/01/the-nicene-creed.

The Transfiguring Power of the Gospel

The brilliance of ethicist and theologian Wyndy Corbin Reuschling helps illumine the path toward wholeness through a renewed understanding of theosis. This patristic concept stems from ancient, Christ-centered wisdom but is often overlooked in the contemporary church. Reuschling's academic and pastoral approach can help us to address our Saulish choices and our relationship with God's transformative love.

Reuschling writes the following:

[Theōsis] must be understood within the entire economy of salvation. Theōsis is not simply the final, ultimate stage in a linear notion of the ordo salutis. Although it is ultimate in the sense that union with God will be fully realized in the future, theōsis infuses and properly orients each element classically understood within the ordo salutis: calling, regeneration, conversion, faith, justification, sanctification, and union with God.[1]

Reuschling situates theosis within the economy of salvation, which is the triune God's comprehensive plan for the redemption of humanity that encompasses all actions, events, and processes through which the Father, Son, and Spirit bring about our salvation. Theosis is integral to the triune God's saving actions in our lives from the beginning. Reuschling argues that it is not a final stage in a linear order of salvation (*ordo salutis*) but (1) a principle that animates our walk in the Spirit and (2) an ongoing process that shapes how we follow Jesus and partake of the triune life.

Reuschling challenges the common suppositions of a sequential spiritual progression that occurs in distinct stages. From her perspective, salvation is an integrated and holistic experience of becoming united with the Father, through the Son, by the Spirit. In contrast to the traditional order of salvation that outlines a salvation sequence of calling, regeneration, conversion, faith, justification, sanctification, and, finally, union with the triune God, Reuschling suggests that although theosis is ultimate in the sense of a fully realized future union with the triune God, it is not confined to the end of this process. Instead, it "infuses and properly orients" every stage of our salvation journey.

Thus, our transformative union with the Father, the Son, and the Spirit is an active and present reality with myriad implications for our lives in Christ. Each aspect of our faith journey is an opportunity for deeper union with the One who has called us out of darkness into his marvelous light. Salvation becomes more than a legal or forensic change in status before God; it is the ongoing reshaping by which we are conformed to the likeness of Christ.

Reuschling contends that "from the start, we have been called to participate in God's divine life in our creaturely existence as stewards, co-creators, and God's image bearers."[2] Think about that! From the outset of creation, humanity has been invited to partake in the divine life as image-bearers, a calling that encompasses every role she mentions. She adds, "The regenerative and redemptive work of the Holy Spirit turns us again to this original calling to be united with God and makes this possible as we grow into the humans God created and called us to be."[3]

We are well aware that the Fall ushered death into the human race because of sin, and as a result, the image of God in us was marred. Yet we have been rehabilitated through the work of the Spirit in redemption and regeneration. The Spirit brings us back into a life of union with the Father, through the mediation of the Incarnate Son. As Reuschling makes clear, "Salvation has never been about "just getting saved."[4] It is not a transactional event aimed to secure our place in heaven after we die. For her, "salvation is the process by which we are redeemed, restored, and recreated to be and become the persons we were meant to be in the first place, in participatory union with God, reflecting what we will perfectly become on the day of God's final and ultimate restoration of all things."[5]

Reuschling also posits that salvation encompasses both our individual restoration and our collective destiny as part of God's creation. This ongoing journey will find its completion in the eschatological reality of God's final restoration of all things. In this view, theosis is both the means and the end of our salvation, encapsulating the theological and moral significance of our transformation into the likeness of Christ, as we anticipate the perfect union with God in the age to come.

Reuschling further articulates that our partaking of the divine nature has to be understood through the lens of Christ's incarnation. Jesus exemplifies the ultimate pattern for theosis, showing us that the true fulfillment of our potential involves becoming more like Christ, who is humanity perfected in God's image. This process, sometimes referred to as *Christification*, suggests that our ultimate destiny is not to alter or escape our human nature but to find its perfection in Christ as we respond to God's grace. Rather than transcending our humanity, we allow it to be transformed through our engagement in God's divine life. This growth into divine likeness occurs as we accept the invitation to partake in the divine nature, as described in 2 Peter 1:3–11.[6]

The Shadow and Theosis: Finding Common Ground

Jung's concept of the shadow and the ancient patristic notion of theosis, which encompasses the stages of purification (purgation), illumination, and union (theosis or deification),[7] are compatible in their understanding of the human journey toward wholeness in the divine image. Although the two frameworks arise from distinct traditions—one psychological and one Christian mystical—each offers insights that speak, from a Christ-centered perspective, to our becoming fully actualized, integrated human beings in communion with the triune God. Let's now briefly explore the traditional stages of theosis.

Purgation/Purification and Confronting the Shadow

This stage of theosis corresponds closely with the Jungian concept of confronting and integrating the shadow. Purgation involves a cleansing or purification of the soul from certain passions and attachments by the work of the indwelling Spirit. These passions and attachments correspond to the darker, repressed, or unacknowledged parts of our psyche. Just as purgation/purification requires us to face our sins, faults, and the aspects of ourselves that are barriers to union with God, confronting the shadow involves recognizing and embracing our inner darkness and complexity. This process is foundational for growth, as it clears the ground for deeper self-knowledge and the spiritual formation that comes by way of the cross-shaped life.

Illumination and Shadow Integration

Following purgation/purification, the stage of illumination in theosis is akin to the integration of the shadow in Jung's framework. Illumination refers to the enlightening of the mind and heart by divine grace, leading to an increased awareness of God's presence and a deeper understanding of the truth as it is in Christ Jesus. Similarly, in analytical psychology, the integration of the shadow is intended to bring about a heightened awareness of the self, where previously unconscious aspects are brought to light and reconciled with the conscious mind. This integration, it is claimed, fosters a more complete, balanced, and authentic self, capable of navigating life with greater wisdom and compassion. In both traditions, this stage is marked by an inner transformation that prepares the soul for a closer communion with God.

Theosis and Individuation

The final stage of theosis, deification, or union with God, bears resemblance to the ultimate goal of Jungian individuation—the realization of the self or the harmonious unification of all aspects of one's personality. In Jung's own words, the Self with a capital "S" is

> a quantity that is supraordinate to the conscious ego. It embraces not only the conscious but also the unconscious psyche, and is therefore, so to speak, a personality which we also are. . . . There is little hope of our ever being able to reach even approximate consciousness of the self, since however much we may make conscious there will always exist an indeterminate and indeterminable amount of unconscious material which belongs to the totality of the self.[8]

In lay terms, Jung introduces the idea of the Self as a vast and comprehensive aspect of our personality that goes far beyond what we typically understand as our conscious identity or ego. Imagine the ego, the "I" with which you identify (including your thoughts, feelings, and decisions), as the tip of an enormous iceberg. This visible tip represents a small portion of your total personality. According to Jung, the bulk of the iceberg, which is submerged and hidden from view, symbolizes the Self. In other words, the Self includes the parts of which you are aware plus a vast expanse of unconscious material. The thoughts, feelings, memories, instincts, ideas, and experiences of which you are not directly conscious nevertheless influence who you are and how you behave.

The challenge, as Jung sees it, is the difficult if not impossible task of knowing the broader Self. Parts of us will always remain hidden within the unconscious. In Jung's view we are much more than we know or can know. This reality invites us to recognize the limitations of our self-knowledge and to remain open to the profound mystery and complexity of who we are.

Much as full awareness is illusive in the Jungian perspective, Christian spirituality suggests that our identity in Christ is an ever-unfolding mystery. We are much more than we can know, not only because there are hidden depths in our psyche but also because of the dynamic process of becoming ever more united with Christ. Theosis, as our mystical union with God, mirrors the psychological journey of individuation in which integration and wholeness are the goals. In theosis, this integration goes beyond the reconciling of our psychic parts; it is about a transformative union with the divine that elevates and sanctifies our entire being. Much like the journey of individuation, the path to union with God involves a continuous process of transformation/transfiguration. Individuation brings the alignment of the ego with the Self, leading to the embodiment of one's truest essence; theosis brings a spiritual alignment by which our will, desires, and nature are incrementally conformed to God's will, desires, and nature. Through this process, we become who we were created to be, realizing our potential as individuals and as bearers of the divine image.

The Christian understanding of identity in Christ adds an almost unfathomable dimension to Jung's concept of the Self. While Jung explores the depths of the unconscious and the process of becoming whole, Christianity points to a wholeness found in relationship with Christ himself. This does not negate the journey of psychological growth but enriches it with a transcendent purpose. In Christ, we find the perfect image of humanity fully alive, and our union with him becomes the ultimate means and end of our growth. The apostle John encapsulates this beautifully when he writes, "Dear friends, now we are children of God, and what we will be has not yet been made known. But we know that when Christ appears, we shall be like him, for we shall see him as he is" (1 John 3:2 NIV).

In Christ, we find not only the archetype of true humanity (John 1:1), but also the promise and power to become fully ourselves (1:12–14), united with the triune God in a *perichoretic dance* of eternal becoming.[9] I would assert, from a Christ-centered perspective, that the ultimate realization of individuation, the complete and holistic integration of our beings, finds its truest expression and possibility in union with Christ.

Personality Numbers 1 and 2

Regarding the parallel processes of theosis and individuation, it is worth noting that Jung sees the *self* as personality number 1 and the *Self* as personality number 2. I want to take a moment to work through the resulting implications. Jung says, "The play and counterplay between personalities No. 1 and No. 2, which has run through my whole life, has nothing to do with a 'split' or dissociation in the ordinary medical sense. On the contrary, it is played out in every individual."[10]

Personality number 1 corresponds to the ego (the extremely limited part of us),[11] our conscious sense of self, encompassing our immediate experiences, thoughts, and actions. It is, in essence, our smaller self, navigating the daily realities of life. Personality number 2, or the Self,[12] represents a deeper, more comprehensive aspect of our being. It is a unifying center that encompasses both the conscious and unconscious realms of our psyche, aiming to harmonize our diverse internal components into a cohesive whole. Jung's process of individuation is the journey toward recognizing and integrating this Self and acknowledging its role in leading us beyond our immediate ego-driven concerns toward a more profound sense of unity and purpose.

In Christ, a parallel yet distinct understanding of the Self emerges from the concept of *imago Dei*—the image of God within us. Galatians 2:20, with its profound declaration of "Christ living in me," offers a rich theological lens through which to view the Self. This verse captures the transformative reality of partaking of the life of Christ and inviting the ego (the smaller self) into a process of cruciformity through the dynamics of death and resurrection. Thus, the Self is not only a psychological center of balance and integration but the indwelling presence of Christ, the perfect image of the invisible God within us.

The dialogue between Jung's concept of individuation and the Christian understanding of theosis reveals both convergence and divergence. Both processes recognize the human being's transformative potential to transcend personal limitations and achieve a state of unity. However, the two processes do not share the same ultimate goal. The Jungian therapy views the Self as the ultimate goal of psychological development; the ultimate goal in the Christian tradition is union with God through Christ, with the Self becoming a vessel for the divine presence.

We can (and in my view we should) acknowledge the value of Jung's contributions to understanding the human psyche while affirming the Christian claim of transformation in Christ. The Christian transformation transcends psychological individuation and is a journey into the heart of God, where the imago Dei within us is fully realized. This distinctive pathway for personal and spiritual growth honors the complexity of the human condition but anchors our hope and identity in the gospel's transfiguring power.

Relating to Contemporary Spiritual Practice

The ancient and modern insights we have explored can inform a holistic approach to personal and spiritual development. By engaging in practices that foster self-examination, repentance, and watchfulness in prayer (purgation and confronting the shadow by the sanctifying presence of the indwelling Spirit), we can cultivate a deeper, more balanced awareness of our limitations and innate potential (illumination and integration). Both individuation and theosis are moves toward a greater state of integration, reconciling those parts of ourselves with which we have been at odds. I am suggesting that the patristic notion of theosis and the Jungian psychology both enrich our understanding of the human quest for wholeness.

The Church's Call to Reform and Individuation

Saul's failure to confront and integrate his inner shadows is no longer a lesson for ancient peoples. It is for us and urges us to seek God's face. Let us do so first in the humility that makes us willing to listen for divine direction and, second, with the courage to face our vulnerabilities and fears. This lesson is crucial for our times, highlighting the importance of remaining open to God's leading, especially when faced with decisions that challenge our convictions and test our faith.

We can see how this journey of self-awareness and confrontation with our shadows can lead us to the practice of resurrection—the practice of living out the reality of Christ's victory over death in our daily lives. This way of living relies on a transformative way of being that is characterized by renewal, hope, and the power of new beginnings. By engaging in the collective and individual work of confronting our shadows through the teachings of Christ and the work of the Spirit, we participate in resurrection life. Simply put, we embody the cruciform pattern of self-giving love and humility, making sacrifices for the sake of others, serving with compassion, and committing ourselves to the cause of justice and love.

As the church faces its current challenges and divisions, the stories of Saul and others help us to see the concept of cruciformity more clearly. By embracing our own process of individuation and the practice of resurrection, we can shine a light into our world's shadows, knowing that our ultimate strength and renewal lie in the resurrected Christ, who calls us to live the reality of his resurrection in every aspect of our lives.

Practicing Resurrection

- Wyndy Corbin Reuschling sees salvation not as a sequence of stages (conversion, faith, justification, sanctification, and union with God) but as an integrated and holistic experience of becoming united with the Father, through the Son, by the Spirit. How might her perspective affect your spiritual journey? How might it ease any sense of striving in your spiritual walk and place more value on the totality of the journey?

- Assuming that salvation is not a mere transactional event aimed at securing your place in heaven after you die, how is your view of salvation expanded? How does it become more meaningful in this life?

- Think about our discussion of the visible tip of the iceberg that represents only a small portion of your total personality. How does the hiddenness of the rest of your being (the thoughts, feelings, memories, instincts, ideas, and experiences of which you are not directly conscious) seem to serve your purposes in the short term? How does it cause more difficulty and pain in the long term? Give examples of both.

Notes

1. Wyndy Corbin Reuschling, "The Means and End in 2 Peter 1:3–11: The Theological and Moral Significance of Theōsis," *Journal of Theological Interpretation* 8/2 (2014): 277.
2. Reuschling, "The Means and End in 2 Peter 1:3–11."
3. Reuschling, "The Means and End in 2 Peter 1:3–11."
4. Reuschling, "The Means and End in 2 Peter 1:3–11."
5. Reuschling, "The Means and End in 2 Peter 1:3–11."
6. Reuschling, "The Means and End in 2 Peter 1:3–11," 277–78.
7. "Orthodox teachers have identified three stages in the process of transformation. Different theologians use different names for the three stages, but there is a general consistency of understanding regarding what happens in each of these stages of spiritual development . . . In this essay I will use the terms *purification, illumination,* and *union* for these stages." F. Gregory Rogers, "Spiritual Direction in the Orthodox Tradition," in *Spiritual Direction and the Care of Souls: A Guide to Christian Approaches and Practices,* ed. Gary W. Moon and David G. Benner (Downers Grove, IL: IVP Academic, 2004), 40.
8. "Carl Jung Depth Psychology: The Life, Work, and Legacy of Carl Jung," *Carl Jung Depth Psychology Blog,* accessed May 16, 2016, https://carljungdepthpsychologysite.blog/2022/07/05/carl-jung-thus-we-can-for-instance-see-ourselves-as-a-persona-without-too-much-difficulty/.
9. "Perichoresis (Gk. πειχώρησις). A term in Neoplatonic anthropology that was used to explain how the soul was intimately united to the body without being confused with it; by means of analogy, Gregory of Nazianzus applied it to the union of the two natures in Jesus Christ . . .

In this sense, it was reused by Byzantine authors who saw in the human composite an analogy of the incarnation . . . Maximus the Confessor developed the concept to explain the unity of the person against the monothelites . . . , using the example of a piece of iron placed in a fire, an example Origen had used to illustrate the union of the soul with the Logos. Following the thought of ps.-Cyril . . . , John of Damascus adopted the term *perichoresis* in an analogous sense for the inseparable, but not confused, union of the three divine persons . . . Thanks to the Latin translation of John of Damascus's *Expositio* made by Burgundio of Pisa, scholastic theology also received the idea under the Latin term *circumincessio*." Basil Studer, "Perichoresis," in *Encyclopedia of Ancient Christianity*, ed. Angelo Di Berardino and James Hoover, trans. Joseph T. Papa, Erik A. Koenke, and Eric E. Hewett (Downers Grove, IL: IVP Academic, 2014), 143.

10. C. G. Jung, *Memories, Dreams, Reflections*, rev. ed., ed. Aniela Jaffé, trans. Richard and Clara Winston (New York: Vintage Books, 1989), 45.

11. "My ego was, in any case, difficult enough for me to grasp. In the first place, I was aware that it consisted of two contradictory aspects: No. 1 and No. 2. Second, in both its aspects my ego was extremely limited, subject to all possible self-deceptions and errors, moods, emotions, passions, and sins. It suffered far more defeats than triumphs, was childish, vain, self-seeking, defiant, in need of love, covetous, unjust, sensitive, lazy, irresponsible, and so on. To my sorrow it lacked many of the virtues and talents I admired and envied in others." Jung, *Memories, Dreams, Reflections*, 57.

12. "The self is not only the centre but also the whole circumference which embraces both conscious and unconscious; it is the centre of this totality, just as the ego is the centre of consciousness." Jung, *Memories, Dreams, Reflections*, 398.

8

Practicing the Art of Discernment

Hebrews 11:1 describes faith as "the substance of things hoped for." This verse reveals that this substance, or *hypostasis*, is not an abstract theoretical construct but a tangible essence that can be sensed and experienced within our being. *Hypostasis* is "a technical term . . . found first in the Greek natural sciences, meaning sediment in a liquid. Behind this is a twofold idea, solidification and visibility, which appears in every use of the word, with one aspect or the other predominating. Thus, in the Greek Bible, *hypostasis* refers in particular to true reality."[1]

This substance of faith is an inner certainty, a palpable assurance that emerges from the promises of God and matures as we journey with him. It is the conviction that what we hope for in him will come to fruition, even if it remains unseen. This assurance is like an anchor, grounding us in the reality of God's promises and the expectation of their fulfillment.

This sense of faith develops into a kind of spiritual intuition, a sixth sense that enables us to discern the divine opportunities and insights our rational minds often overlook or dismiss. It is more than a belief in the unseen, however. Nurtured by our ongoing communion with the triune God and our participation in his triune life, this intuitive aspect of faith becomes a tangible, experiential, guiding force. It allows us to sense the divine promises and rest assured in them, freeing us to seize even fleeting moments of divine opportunity with confidence.

The substance of faith far exceeds optimism or positive thinking. It is a profound trust in what is yet unseen. Faith, in its truest sense, is a foundational pillar undergirded and energized by love and raised high by hope. Because Christ is its Author and Finisher, our faith remains confident in the pull of the future. For it is Christ himself who calls us forward from there.

This kind of faith is (1) a fruit of participating in communion with the triune God, and (2) when necessary, a charismatic gift that energizes us and empties us of doubt when we are called to be intentional and act in an instant.

Resilience in Real Life and Beyond

In my college years, I read Carlos Castaneda's works on Don Juan Matus, a fictional Yaqui warrior. The Yaquis "have their roots in Mexico" and were "influenced by Jesuit priests who appeared in their area."[2] As a "sun oriented" people who considered sacred a cross "representing the cardinal points of the Earth and the center of creation,"[3] they were open to the cross-carrying Spanish Jesuit missionaries who "first appeared in Yaqui territory in 1617. . . . For 150 years the Yaquis and the Spaniards lived peacefully with one other, until 1767, when the Jesuits were expelled from the region and Mexican military forces were sent in to conquer the land."[4]

The Mexican military committed great acts of violence against the Yaqui people, destroying their crops and villages and killing many of the people.[5] The methods employed against the Yaquis were appallingly brutal. Policies of extermination included mass executions of men, women, and children by firing squads. Yaquis who were found trying to escape were killed on the spot.

This historical context is important to Castaneda's works, particularly his portrayal of Don Juan Matus. Though many doubt the existence of Don Juan Matus, Castaneda's narratives nevertheless convey a story of resilience and survival against seemingly insurmountable odds.[6]

In his own way Reepicheep, one of the Talking Mice from Narnia, is a character of intriguing contrasts. In the 2010 film *The Voyage of the Dawn Treader*, his unique blend of cantankerousness and affable charm entertained and encouraged moviegoers. Small in stature, Reepicheep nevertheless exudes a sense of fearlessness. Driven by his steadfast commitment to honor, both in regard to himself and others, he is a memorable and compelling figure in the narrative.

Filmmakers took creative liberties by attributing to Reepicheep certain lines not found in C. S. Lewis's writings. A notable example is Reepicheep's line, "Hardships often prepare ordinary people for an extraordinary destiny."[7] Though not a line by Lewis, it resonates with the essence of Reepicheep and his approach to life.

As did the Yaqui people in Castaneda's works, Reepicheep mirrors the characteristics of resilience. Reepicheep's fearless approach to adversity, his willingness to confront dangers head-on, and his acknowledgment of his physical limitations reflect the essence of resilience. It is about more than recovery or survival; resilience involves growth, learning, and transformation in the face of hardship.

In fiction and real life, resilience encompasses endurance, flexibility, and the ability to evolve positively despite adverse circumstances.

Characters like Reepicheep (with their mixture of bravery and practical wisdom) and people like the Yaquis (with their extraordinary and enduring perseverance) demonstrate how resilience shapes one's journey, often preparing individuals for extraordinary destinies.

Not Only Surviving but Emerging Again

This story of survival becomes particularly poignant when considering the fate of the Yaqui people. Those who survived the atrocities were often regarded as "intruders on borrowed land" in regions like "Arizona, New Mexico, California, and Texas."[8] Castaneda's work captures the Yaquis' extreme persecution and marginalization.

The resilience of the Yaquis, highlighted in Castaneda's narratives, is a vivid illustration of resilience as a fundamental human trait. Resilience is the capacity to withstand and adapt to life's adversities, challenges, and changes. It's about bouncing back from difficulties, but it's also more than just recovery. Resilience involves growth, learning, and transformation in the face of hardship. It's a dynamic process that encompasses endurance, flexibility, and the ability to evolve positively despite adverse circumstances.

In the story of the Yaqui, resilience emerges not only as a survival strategy but as a profound expression of cultural strength and spiritual depth. The fact that the Yaqui people embraced the Catholic tradition and Jesuit teachings implies an embrace of Christ's salvation. In any case, their resilience manifests in their ability to maintain their identity and values despite the extreme and debilitating pressures they faced. Their ability to endure and adapt is a testament to their inner strength and the robustness of their cultural and spiritual foundations.

Resilience is crucial in life because it empowers people and communities to navigate the complexities and unpredictability of our world. It's about developing the mental and emotional toughness to face challenges head-on. But it's also about possessing the wisdom to know when to adapt and change course. Resilience is intertwined with hope and optimism, providing the fortitude to envision a better future, even in the bleakest of times.

The Yaquis' resilience is a beacon of inspiration. It demonstrates how people can preserve their dignity, uphold their values, and remain true to their identities when trouble comes. The Yaquis are exemplars of resilience. Their history reminds us that resilience not only helps us to survive life's challenges; it enables us to emerge from them with a renewed sense of purpose and strength. In an often harsh and unforgiving world, resilience keeps us moving forward and finding meaning even in the midst of trials.

Resilience and Resurrection

If we consider the concept of "practicing resurrection" in relation to the Yaqui people, we elevate it beyond a metaphor for human resilience and enter the realm of spiritual and theological significance. To embrace saving faith in Christ is to experience from the inside out an essential transformation that is rooted in the resurrection of Jesus, through the work of the cross.

Faith in Christ is about the profound hope and renewal found in Christ's victory over death and sin. It speaks to a faith that transcends the trials and sufferings of this world, anchored in the promise of eternal life and redemption. In this context, the resilience and survival of the Yaqui people can be seen as an embodiment of the Christian hope. Their endurance in the face of persecution and their ability to maintain their faith amid hardship reflect the transformative power of the resurrection. This is a journey of faith that mirrors the Paschal Mystery—the passion, death, and resurrection of Jesus—which lies at the heart of the faith once and for all delivered to the saints.

Thus, for the Yaquis, practicing resurrection would imply relying on the Spirit's strength and renewal from the inside-out, holding onto hope amid suffering, and experiencing the transformative power of God's love when life seems to be at its darkest. It's a testament to their spiritual resilience, rooted in the faith that has been integrated into their cultural identity and sustained them through their history.

Quiet and the Element of Chance

The resilience and spiritual fortitude of the Yaqui people, shaped by their deep-rooted faith, align remarkably with the philosophy presented in Carlos Castaneda's *Journey to Ixtlan*. Here, Castaneda introduces the "cubic centimeter of chance."[9] He writes,

> All of us, whether or not we are warriors, have a cubic centimeter of chance that pops out in front of our eyes from time to time. The difference between an average man and a warrior is that the warrior is aware of this, and one of his tasks is to be alert, deliberately waiting, so that when his cubic centimeter pops out he has the necessary speed, the prowess, to pick it up.[10]

The metaphor of the cubic centimeter of chance is a potent reminder of the subtle yet profound ways in which the Spirit of God sometimes communicates. It suggests that divine guidance and insight can often manifest in moments of pregnant silence, rather than in grand, resounding declarations. This silence, rich with potential and depth, requires a heightened sensitivity and attentiveness to discern the thunderous silence of the Spirit amid the cacophony of everyday life. In this often overlooked or undervalued quietude lies the profound power of spiritual revelation.

The soldier of the cross, therefore, must cultivate an extraordinary vigilance, a keenness of perception that is attuned to the subtlest of signals. This is not merely about sharpening our senses; it is about honing a habit of attention that permeates our entire being. In the guidance of our paths by the Spirit, this principle manifests as an unyielding focus on Christ, coupled with an ever-ready awareness to discern his presence in the small, often overlooked details of our everyday experiences. It is a quality of attention that demands a heart and mind that are both still and receptive.

In the film *The Bodyguard*,[11] Frank Farmer, portrayed by Kevin Costner, is tasked with protecting Whitney Houston's character, Rachel Marron. In a tense scene set in a remote cabin in the forest, Frank relies not on his sight but his acute sense of hearing to detect the presence of a stalker. He drops to the ground in the snow to listen for any movement, illustrating a profound level of attentiveness and alertness.

This cinematic depiction can be likened to the perfecting of our spiritual senses. The indwelling Spirit of Christ trains us, as we are yielded, to develop a similar acuity in discerning his movements. In the ancient faith, this was understood as *watchfulness*. Consider these words from Bernard of Clairvaux, in speaking of the inner experience of how the spiritual senses are perfected as we cooperate with the indwelling Spirit: "Let the soul be watchful then, if it desires Christ to dwell by faith in its heart, that is, within itself; let it take great care that its members, that is, reason, will, and memory, are not at variance with each other."[12]

Bernard of Clairvaux's wisdom implores us to ensure harmony within our souls, emphasizing the alignment of reason, will, and memory as a prerequisite for communion with the indwelling Christ. This call for internal coherence serves as a foundation for a deeper spiritual journey. It is not merely about the absence of conflict among these faculties, but their active collaboration toward a singular, divine intent.

As we consider the disciplined practice of abiding, this unity within ourselves becomes increasingly significant. It is through deliberate and sustained effort that we start recognizing the nuances of our internal dynamics. This recognition is the first step toward adjusting our internal posture. It involves a holistic transformation that encompasses our way of thinking (reason), our intentions and desires (will), and our recollections and understanding of experiences (memory).

Over time, this harmonious interaction fosters a more profound awareness of our spiritual needs. It prompts fundamental shifts in how we perceive the world (seeing), how we interpret and understand (listening), and how we interact and express ourselves (speaking and acting). Such shifts are not superficial changes but are indicative of a deeper metamorphosis within the core of our being.

Bernard of Clairvaux's counsel sets the stage for a transformative journey. It is a journey of becoming, where disciplined practice refines and realigns our inner faculties. This process is not instantaneous but evolves over time, through consistent and watchful practice. It is in this disciplined journey of internal alignment and adjustment that we find the pathway to a more profound spiritual existence, where Christ's presence within us becomes more palpable and influential in every aspect of our lives.

Over time, then, and through the disciplined practice of abiding, we become more aware of our need to adjust our internal posture and our will, and make fundamental shifts in our way of seeing, our way of listening, and our way of speaking and acting. As we make these fundamental internal shifts, discernment sharpens, and we are more able to distinguish and discriminate between the subtle ways in which the Spirit breathes into our lives as opposed to the aggressive pushing and driving of the forces of darkness.

A. W. Tozer weighs in on the issue of stillness, saying,

> Our fathers had much to say about stillness, and by stillness they meant the absence of motion or the absence of noise or both.

They felt that they must be still for at least a part of the day, or that day would be wasted. God can be known in the tumult of the world if His providence has for the time placed us there, but He is known best in the silence. So they held, and so the sacred Scriptures declare. Inward assurance comes out of the stillness. We must be still to know.[13]

A. W. Tozer's profound insight into the value of stillness as a means to deeper spiritual understanding serves as a foundational concept that connects seamlessly with the practice of discernment in our daily lives. Tozer emphasizes that while God can indeed be known amid life's tumult, there is a special clarity and depth of understanding that emerges in the quiet and stillness. This concept of stillness as a gateway to inward assurance and deeper knowledge of God sets the stage for how we approach the practice of discernment.

In the quiet, unassuming moments of life, away from the noise and distractions, we learn to practice discernment as we meditate on Scripture and bring our meditations to speech in prayer before the triune God with whom we commune. Just as Frank Farmer's keen listening in the snow represents a heightened state of awareness, our spiritual sensitivity allows us to hear the resounding silence of the Spirit's voice amid the noise and clamor of our surroundings. The discipline of abiding cultivates in us an ability to perceive the divine presence and guidance in the seemingly small and ordinary aspects of our daily lives, guiding us in a way that is not forceful or domineering, but subtle and convincing.

This analogy serves to remind us that in our spiritual walk, the most profound encounters with God often come not in the loud and dramatic, but in the still, fertile silence of the Spirit. It's in this attuned state of being that we find the true course of our journey with Christ, led not by external pressures, but by the muted, patterned, immovable witness and guidance of the Holy Spirit within us. This state of heightened awareness is more than a passive waiting; it is an active, dynamic engagement with the space we occupy within and without.

Furthermore, seizing that "cubic centimeter of chance" implies a readiness to act. It's one thing to notice divine opportunities; it's another to respond to them with courage and faith. This means stepping out in faith, even when the path is not fully clear, trusting that Christ is leading us into deeper waters of understanding and experience.

In essence, as we partake of the very fellowship of the Son of God (1 Cor. 1:9), we develop that necessary quality of holy attention that is rare and refined. It calls for a perpetual, observant awareness of God's presence in our lives, a readiness to hear his voice in our depths, and the courage to act on the opportunities he presents. This journey is not for the faint of heart. It is a path marked by deep-seated engagement, single-minded focus, and a profound desire to encounter and embrace the infinitesimal yet transformative moments that God, in his grace, places in our paths. Such deliberate waiting is an active, expectant posture. It's not a passive waiting but a keen, prayerful watchfulness. It's about being ready to act when God opens a door, presents an opportunity, or calls us to a particular task. This readiness doesn't come overnight; it's cultivated in our participation with Christ moment by moment, by the grace of the indwelling Spirit, and our ruminating on the sacred text.

So when that cubic centimeter of chance does appear—that divine appointment, that opportunity to redeem the kairos moment (Eph. 5:16–18)—we are prepared to seize it with the speed and prowess of a spiritual warrior. Jesus is clear that we are to live lives that are "dressed in readiness" (Luke 12:35 NASB1995) so that we can have the "necessary prowess" to "pick up" the cubic centimeter of chance. Think about how infinitely small a cubic centimeter is and the significant quality of attention you would need to even see it when it presents itself!

This has to be something you intend with all your heart. There has to be a serious and Spirit-wrought assurance that goes beyond easy-believism or superficial optimism. This faith, intertwined with hope and love, becomes a powerful force, guiding us through the complexities of our world with a perspective that transcends the immediate and the apparent.

Seizing the Moment: The Opportune

Embracing the cubic centimeter of chance requires more than mere readiness. Ephesians 5:16–18 speaks of "redeeming the time," which in the original Greek refers to seizing the kairos[14]—the opportune, God-appointed moments. These are not just chronological instances but are charged with potential and purpose, laden with the possibility of transformation and growth. Eric White goes to great lengths to explain the kairos moment:

> Kairos is an ancient Greek word that means "the right moment'"
> or "the opportune." The two meanings of the word apparently
> come from two different sources. In archery, it refers to an open-
> ing, or "opportunity" or, more precisely, a long tunnel-like aper-
> ture through which the archer's arrow has to pass.[15]

In this context, our preparedness to act must be undergirded by a robust spiritual foundation. It is not enough to simply be alert; we must cultivate a quality of attention that is attuned to the subtle movements of the Spirit. This attentiveness is akin to a spiritual warrior's skill, honed through disciplined practice and a deep connection with God. Such prowess as that of an archer enables us to discern the significance of fleeting moments that, though small like a cubic centimeter, hold immense potential for impact in our lives and the lives of others.

White continues by sharing, "Successful passage of a kairos requires, therefore, that the archer's arrow be fired not only accurately but with enough power for it to penetrate."[16] Furthermore, this readiness and discernment must be rooted in a sincere intentionality. This commitment engages the whole heart with an unwavering resolve that stems from a Spirit-led assurance. This is not a shallow feel-good belief system or an optimistic outlook. Instead, this faith intertwines hope and love and refines the vision with which we navigate a complex world. Instead of acknowledging divine moments, it actively seeks them, recognizes them, and responds to them with courage and conviction.

This can be seen in White's approach to the secondary meaning of kairos from the ancient Greek concept:

> The second meaning of kairos traces to the art of weaving. There it is "the critical time" when the weaver must draw the yarn through a gap that momentarily opens in the warp of the cloth being woven. Putting the two meanings together, one might understand kairos to refer to a passing instant when an opening appears which must be driven through with force if success is to be achieved.[17]

White's exploration of kairos and its application in weaving evokes a parallel to the art of knitting that my grandmothers practiced so skillfully. Their precision resonates with the idea of seizing the opportune moment. As White describes it, kairos represents that critical time when the weaver must draw the yarn through a momentary gap in the warp of the cloth. In my grandmothers' knitting, I saw more than a mechanical form of repetition; I saw their embodied knowledge and intuitive timing as they slid their needles in a perfect rhythm. It was an art form in which each loop and stitch was opportune and mirrored the concept of kairos.

There is a parallel here to the practice of faith that becomes an intrinsic part of our being through rehearsal and repetition. Our continual engagement in prayer, service, study, and meditation develops our spiritual muscle memory. As our sensitivity to the divine timing increases, our responses to Kairos moments become more instinctual and attuned the divine rhythm. This is the essence of living in kairos.

In practicing our faith, we cultivate perspectives that transcend what is immediate and apparent. Kairos moments become opportunities to manifest God's kingdom in the here and now—not just seizing opportunities as they arise but allowing such moments to shape us into vessels more aligned with God's will and purpose. This challenges us to live in an active state of readiness with our "lamps lit" (Luke 12:35), ready to embrace each kairos moment with the fullness of our faith, hope, and love.

These reflections bring to mind the work of Martin Buber, particularly in the context of practicing resurrection. In his seminal work *I and Thou*, the depth of Buber's insights requires careful contemplation. One of the most profound in relation to our subject resonates deeply:

> The free man is he who wills without arbitrary self-will. He believes in reality, that is, he believes in the real solidarity of the real twofold entity 1 and Thou. He believes in destiny, and believes that it stands in need of him. It does not keep him in leading-strings, it awaits him, he must go to it, yet does not know where it is to be found. But he knows that he must go out with his whole being. The matter will not turn out according to his decision; but what is to come will come only when he decides on what he is able to will. He must sacrifice his puny, unfree will, that is controlled by things and instincts, to his grand will, which quits, defined for destined being. Then he intervenes no more, but at the same time he does not let things merely happen. He listens to what is emerging from himself, to the course of

being in the world; not in order to be supported by it, but in order to bring it to reality as it desires, in its need of him, to be brought—with human spirit and deed, human life and death.[18]

Here Buber opens a window on our engagement with the cubic centimeter of chance and the concept of kairos. His vision of the free person echoes our call to be dressed in readiness. In Buber's eyes, the free person exercises will not for arbitrary self-interest but in consonance with the profound "I and Thou" relationship. This person recognizes and engages with destiny, not as a predetermined path but as an active, purposeful journey—not driven by instinct or external pressures but motivated by a grander vision of what it means to live a destined life. This involves a sense of mystery and an openness to the unfolding of events, yet it is rooted in intentional participation, as in the seizing of kairos moments.

Kairos, then, is not just a moment in chronological time but a significant opportunity laden with meaning and purpose. To seize it is to align our will with a greater narrative, to fulfill a role that goes beyond the immediate and transient. It is about contributing to the grand narrative of God's eternal purpose in a way that is both meaningful and transformative.

Had King Saul surrendered his "puny unfree will" to the grand will of Yahweh, how might things have turned out? Instead of succumbing to insecurity and the attendant disaster of a fear-based complex, Saul could have celebrated David as a son and not a rival. Instead of tormenting David, he could have embraced him as a mentor would. Yahweh could have positioned Saul to participate not only in his own destiny but, as a pivotal figure, in the collective destiny of Israel. Instead of being remembered for his failings, he might have been marked as the greatest king in its history.

Buber's sense of the human will being integrated with divine destiny speaks of true freedom and fulfillment. It urges us to move beyond our limited, reactive impulses to engage with a higher, "grand will" and, therefore, a more meaningful purpose. Our active participation in the divine plan is then woven into the tapestry of our collective existence.

Buber's concepts speak soundly to the idea of practicing resurrection. Our engagement with the world, destiny, and God transcends happenstance and isolated decisions. It represents a continuous journey of aligning our will with the truths of our existence and the call of destiny. On this journey, the kairos moments we embrace shape our identity and spiritual evolution.

Practicing resurrection is the active embodiment of hope, renewal, and transformation that mirrors the resurrection of Christ. This practice is not confined to moments of spiritual contemplation but is part of our daily lives. With hearts attuned to the deeper rhythms of God's purpose, we are free to seize kairos moments and find the essences of resurrection—a continual process of dying to the old and emerging anew with divine purpose and direction. Thus, our choices, actions, and responses are a dance with destiny, and each step, each movement, is an act of practicing resurrection.

Practicing Resurrection

- The substance of faith is an inner certainty that emerges from the promises of God and matures as we walk with him. How has this assurance served as an anchor during a difficult season in your life? Were you consciously aware that you were anchored at the time, or did the realization come later? How might your response(s) influence you in the future?

- Resilience is about developing the mental and emotional toughness to face challenges head-on. But it's also about possessing the wisdom to know when to adapt and change course. What is the hardest part of confronting your difficulties? What is the hardest part of adapting and changing course?

- The disciplined practice of abiding makes us more aware of our internal posture and any adjustments we need to make regarding our will, ways of seeing and listening, and ways of speaking and acting. Reflect on an experience in which you made these fundamental internal shifts. How were you enabled to sense the Spirit's subtle way of breathing into your life?

Notes

1. Studer, "Hypostasis," in *Encyclopedia of Ancient Christianity*, 308.
2. Lavonna L. Lovern and Carol Locust, *Native American Communities on Health and Disability* (New York: Palgrave Macmillan, 2013), 113.
3. Lovern and Locust, *Native American Communities on Health and Disability*, 113.
4. Lovern and Locust, *Native American Communities on Health and Disability*, 113–14.
5. Lovern and Locust, *Native American Communities on Health and Disability*, 114.
6. Lovern and Locust, *Native American Communities on Health and Disability*, 114.
7. William OFlaherty, "(CCSLQ-1) Hardships Often Prepare," Essential C. S. Lewis, last updated May 5, 2018, https://essentialcslewis.com/2015/08/29/hardships-often-prepare-ordinary-people/.
8. Lovern and Locust, *Native American Communities on Health and Disability*, 114.
9. Carlos Castaneda, *Journey to Ixtlan: The Lessons of Don Juan* (New York: Simon & Schuster, 1972), 138.
10. Castaneda, *Journey to Ixtlan*, 138.
11. *The Bodyguard*, directed by Mick Jackson (Burbank, CA: Warner Bros., 1992).
12. Bernard of Clairvaux, *Sermons for the Autumn Season*, Cistercian Fathers Series, trans. Irene Edmonds and Mark Scott, vol. 54 (Collegeville, MN: Liturgical Press, 2016), 186.

13. A. W. Tozer, *Tozer on the Almighty God: A 365-Day Devotional*, compiled by Ron Eggert (Chicago: Moody Publishers, 2004), 6.

14. Stanley Grenz, David Guretzki, and Cherith Fee Nordling, *Pocket Dictionary of Theological Terms* (Downers Grove, IL: InterVarsity Press, 1999), 69–70.

15. Eric Charles White, *Kaironomia: On the Will-to-Invent* (Ithaca, NY: Cornell University Press, 1987), [page #].

16. White, *Kaironomia*.

17. White, *Kaironomia*.

18. Martin Buber, *I and Thou*, trans. Ronald Gregor Smith (Edinburgh: T&T Clark, 1937), 59–60.

9

Embracing the Journey

Eighteenth-century writer and avid letter-writer Horace Walpole coined the term *serendipity* in a letter to a British diplomat with whom he corresponded for forty-five years.[1] Although Walpole was a Cambridge graduate and the son of a British prime minister, his own career was said to be "undistinguished."[2] Yet his coining of a word left his mark on the English language.

The term was not wholly original. Walpole was inspired by the tale of *The Three Princes of Serendip*,[3] which told of the princes' journey and the ways in which fortuitous discoveries marked their adventures even as their intentional actions did. Walpole explained that the princes "were always making discoveries, by accidents and sagacity, of things they were not in quest of."[4] This beautifully mirrors our own spiritual journeys, where, despite our plans and intentions, we often encounter important truths and revelations in the most unforeseen circumstances.

In the context of faith, serendipity is not all about happy accidents or chance encounters; it is about recognizing the hand of the Almighty in our daily experiences. Serendipitous moments often arrive in the guise of "valuable or agreeable things not sought for,"[5] challenging us to peer beyond the surface and discern the deeper workings of Providence in our lives.

Consciously realizing how these unexpected moments of discovery and insight enrich our understanding of faith, destiny, and our relationship with God is important. Just as the practice of resurrection and the seizing of kairos moments require an openness to the Spirit's leading, serendipity requires a heart attuned to the possibilities that lie beyond our immediate vision. Walpole said that the princes were "always making discoveries, by accidents and sagacity."[6] *Sagacity* is wisdom, by the way. Walpole was stressing that recognizing accidental discoveries demands a quality of perception along the way.

From a scriptural perspective, we could say that if we will "count it all joy" as we "encounter various trials" (James 1:2), wisdom will be given!

The Seemingly Recent Yet Long-Ago Past

When Twentieth Century Fox released its remake of the 1947 film *The Secret Life of Walter Mitty*, fans of Ben Stiller (like me) were drawn in by a trailer that promised a movie packed with humor, adventure, and heart. Stiller not only starred in the film but also directed it.

The story is about *Life* magazine's negative asset manager Walter Mitty, whose life is filled with dull routines and grand daydreams of adventure.[7] Then the disappearance of a photo negative that is crucial to the magazine's final print issue upends his unremarkable journey and sends him on a global quest to find elusive photographer Sean O'Connell and the missing image.

Walter is unceremoniously thrust out of his New York City envi-
rons and into the icy landscapes of Greenland, the volcanic realities of
Iceland, and the majesty of the Himalayas. Along the way he experiences a series of challenges and serendipitous events that awaken him
to the joys and possibilities of a life beyond his imagination.[8]

The journey transforms Walter, imbuing him with confidence and
a zest for life he had previously experienced only in his fantasies. He
learns the importance of being present in the moment. He embraces
the unknown. And he begins to live his life to the fullest. The transformation is not only internal; it touches his outlook and relationships
and reveals the powerful impact of stepping into the unknown.[9]

The movie was timely, emerging when themes of adventure,
self-discovery, and breaking free of the digital echo chamber had a
certain resonance. Walter's journey reminded moviegoers of their
potential to transform their lives through bold choices and genuine experiences. Reviews of the film were mixed, but a considerable
audience embraced its heartwarming and inspiring message of self-
discovery and adventure.

Cinematic Signs of the Times

Measured by its impact on viewers and its awareness of the signs of the
times, *The Secret Life of Walter Mitty* was unforgettable. It touched on
many aspects of contemporary life and presented the hope of individual (and ultimately collective) awakening. Let's take a quick look at
some of its twenty-first-century themes.

Virtual versus Real Life and Authenticity

By 2013, people had become increasingly absorbed in their digital lives,
so the film's message of engaging with the real world and real adventures struck a chord. It contrasted the idea of living vicariously through

media consumption and online personas with the prospect of actively participating in real-life experiences. It advocated a kind of awakening, not only to lived experiences but to a resurrected authenticity.

Curated portrayals of life via social media made life seem progressively superficial. Walter Mitty's departure from daydreams to actual adventures inspired us to seek personal growth beyond the digital façade and reminded us that authenticity mattered.

Economic Uncertainty and Personal Choices

The lingering impact of the 2007–2008 financial crisis caused many people to reevaluate their life choices, careers, and the pursuit of material success over personal fulfillment. *The Secret Life of Walter Mitty* encouraged viewers to contemplate these themes, suggesting that courage, adventure, and self-discovery could lead them beyond conventional success and into the realm of personal fulfillment.

Reflecting on Life's Purpose

The rethinking that followed severe economic pressures led to universal questions about life's purpose and the pursuit of dreams. The movie tapped into the zeitgeist and encouraged reflection—on choosing paths, making more inspired decisions, and not letting fear and complacency hinder our higher aspirations.

In capturing all of this, Ben Stiller took the audience on the epic monomyth, the hero's journey, the universal quest beyond self-imposed boundaries, where meaning, purpose, and dream fulfillment can be actualized. As a narrative of transformation and the pursuit of the extraordinary, the movie provided a seamless transition into the realm of serendipity.

This realm is exemplified in the biblical story of Saul's quest for his father's lost donkeys. Just as Walter Mitty's journey from the confines of mundane existence to the expanses of the unknown leads him to his true self and purpose, Saul's seemingly ordinary task sets the stage for divine intervention and the unfolding of his destiny. Both stories show how unexpected events can steer us toward unimagined futures while urging us to remain open to the possibilities that serendipity reveals.

In Saul's case, the search for lost donkeys becomes much more than a simple errand; it becomes a pivot point ordained by Yahweh, and it leads to Saul's being anointed as Israel's first king. Whether it's the pursuit of a missing photograph or the search for lost animals, such quests invite us to explore the unknown, embrace serendipity, and discover our place within a much larger story that is playing out all around us. As we do, we realize that the path of purpose is paved with moments of unexpected grace and unimagined opportunity.

Cinematic Escape and Inspiration

Amid the always-developing backdrop of global challenges, *The Secret Life of Walter Mitty* offered both an escape and a wellspring of inspiration. Not only did its philosophical message refresh our mindsets, but its breathtaking visuals lifted us from the familiar with reminders of our planet's expansive beauty.

Where Is God in All of This?

As followers of Jesus, we are invited to view serendipitous events through the lens of faith, trusting in the inherent goodness of God and his intention for us. This trust does not blind us to reality; it sharpens our ability to perceive God's hand in the unexpected and seemingly random events of our lives.

Faith invites our openness to the hidden treasures that lie along our paths. Faith requires us to cultivate an expectancy amid life's uncertainty and unknowns, holding firm to the belief that God is at work. Our embrace of serendipity reveals that life is not a random series of events but a meaningful narrative filled with purpose and promise. Saul's quest for lost donkeys led him to a "cubic centimeter of chance"[10]—a pivotal encounter with Yahweh's prophet Samuel. Likewise, our collective journeys through troubled times lead us toward unforeseen wisdom and hidden paths of renewal.

This truth doesn't trivialize or ignore the gravity of the evils and sorrows we are facing. It reminds us that in navigating our darkest nights, we often stumble on the most illuminating insights. If our hearts remain open in the current milieu of challenge and opportunity, we can become "perfect and complete, lacking nothing" (Jas. 1:4).

Saul's Quest

When Kish realized that his donkeys were lost, he "said to his son Saul, 'Take now with you one of the young men, and arise, go search for the donkeys'" (1 Sam. 9:3). In every culture, people pursue lost elements to which they attribute great value. I am reminded of something I read years ago in Joseph Chilton Pearce's book, *The Crack in the Cosmic Egg*: "The asking of an ultimately serious question, which means to be seized in turn by an ultimately serious quest, reshapes our concepts in favor of the kinds of perceptions needed to 'see' the desired answer."[11]

Can we find in Pearce's insight a parallel to Saul's quest to find his father's lost donkeys? I think so. The notion that an earnest quest reshapes our perceptions so we can discern the answer we are seeking resonates with Saul's assignment from his father. Saul does not know the search is about more than the physical retrieval of lost animals. He has no clue that it's about the transformative journey he is about to undergo. He cannot imagine that his journey will require a deepening of his own self-awareness.

Saul does know that his quest is tied to the noble qualities expressed by the first commandment with a promise: "Honor your father and mother, so that you may live long in the land the LORD your God is giving you" (Exod. 20:12 NIV). Embedded deep in Saul's core is a value system centered on honoring his father, Kish. It is more than a religious obligation; it is part of the cultural and ethical foundation that Saul upholds—a foundation we would do well to rebuild in the current culture.

In his earnest pursuit to honor his father's concerns, Saul exemplifies respect, love, and loyalty to the principles of this commandment. His willingness to embark on the search for donkeys and face whatever uncertainty and challenges might arise testifies to the reverence he attaches to his father's wishes. Saul's quest is more than a task; it is a sacred duty driven by a sense of responsibility that exceeds the material value of the lost donkeys and expresses his commitment to fulfilling his father's expectations.

Disconnect? What Disconnect?

As creatures brought forth from the earth on the sixth day of creation (Gen. 1:24), donkeys have an instinctual nature. Isaiah concurs, writing that "an ox knows its owner, and a donkey its master's manger" (Isa. 1:3). He then laments, "But Israel does not know; my people do not perceive" (1:3). The juxtaposition of the instinctual knowledge of animals and the spiritual forgetfulness of God's people is stirring and relatable in our twenty-first-century context.

Consider the fact that we are daily overwhelmed with data—more in a day than what individuals in antiquity would have processed in whole lifetimes. Yet have we maintained an instinctual connection to our Creator, as the oxen and donkeys have done? Or are we, in our sophistication, disconnected from the One who sustains us, like the people whom Isaiah laments? Donkeys will instinctually find their way back to their master's manger, but despite our technological prowess and abundance of information, we may be more lost than we ever were.

Isaiah's critique of Israel's forgetfulness and lack of perception eerily presages our current age. Despite the advancements that set us apart from the ancient world, our fundamental challenge remains the same: to know and recognize our Source, our Creator. Ironically enough, we find ourselves profoundly disconnected from each other and from the triune God—in an age that is defined by connectivity. This breach invites us to reflect on our spiritual instincts. Are we so immersed in our pursuit of information and technology that we overlook our basic, instinctual awareness of relationship with God? Do we suppose that our pursuit is valid, or has it become an outlet for our tendency to run from God? Is that what drives our preoccupation? Are we using it (consciously or not) to ease away from our most vital connection?

From Vulnerable to Resilient

Saul's initial anxiety over lost donkeys and his subsequent encounter with Samuel accent a transition from a state of perceived vulnerability to one of potential resilience. Facing the uncertainty of his mission and the weight of familial expectations, Saul embodies the anxiety that his sense of vulnerability generates. Yet as the narrative unfolds, an alternative path appears and draws him into an unexpected and daunting role. This critical moment of choice underscores Kevin Bingaman's assertion that our ability to recognize the choices before us is contingent on our self-perception—specifically, whether we see ourselves as defined by our vulnerability or by our capacity for resilience.[12]

This choice involves the ways in which our internal narratives guide our decisions when life's unpredictable twists and turns create pressure. Whether it is anchored in vulnerability or resilience, our self-perception influences more than our decision-making; it forms the contours of our journey. Recognizing our vulnerabilities is not inherently self-defeating. A healthy assessment of our vulnerabilities is necessary to personal growth, fostering empathy and connection with others. Nurturing our resilience empowers us to confront challenges with strength and adaptability, turning potential setbacks into opportunities for learning and evolution.

Because we can assign too much power to our vulnerabilities, we need to make a conscious effort to reframe our encounters with adversity. Instead of viewing them as insurmountable obstacles, we can see them as chances to expand our horizons and develop deeper self-awareness. This requires self-reflection and an openness to changing the story we tell ourselves about ourselves.

For better or worse, that story reflects our perceptions of self, which themselves are affected by external factors. Societal expectations, cultural norms, and the opinions of others influence how we see ourselves. Therefore, they affect the menu of choices we see as being available to us. When this menu is obscured, the serendipitous opportunities that reveal themselves along the way also become obscured. However, we can consciously reclaim our sense of agency and expand our perception of available choices. This reclamation means examining the external pressures that affect our self-perception and consciously suspending their unconscious impacts. Rather than succumbing to prescribed or less promising paths, we can see ourselves more objectively and align our decisions with our authentic, more adventurous selves.

Fostering resilience becomes key when navigating life's unpredictable waters. The practice of abiding in Christ is essential. So is developing a quality of attention that stems from communing with God, cultivating supportive relationships in Christ, and engaging in reflective self-dialogue. These practices can strengthen our ability to face the unknown courageously, optimistically, and, most importantly, faithfully. The resilience we cultivate enhances our capacity to recognize serendipitous opportunities and enables us to pursue them. In this way, we transform our vulnerabilities into strengths.

The Seer and the Would-Be King

Seeing and looking are not quite the same. In looking, one might observe this or that. But in seeing, one can discern what *this* and *that* are about. The prophet Samuel both observed and saw. His seeing not only established his name in Israel but also confirmed his call in the people's eyes. Samuel was a formative figure in the lives of those he served and mentored. He was certainly essential in Saul's ascension to the throne.

> Now a day before Saul's coming [to Zuph], Yahweh had revealed this in Samuel's hearing, saying, "About this time tomorrow I will send you a man from the land of Benjamin, and you shall anoint him to be ruler over My people Israel; and he will save My people from the hand of the Philistines. For I have regarded My people because their cry has come to Me." Now Samuel saw Saul, and Yahweh answered him, "Behold, the man of whom I spoke to you! This one shall restrict My people." Then Saul approached Samuel in the gate and said, "Please tell me where the seer's house is." And Samuel answered Saul and said, "I am the seer. Go up before me to the high place, for you shall eat with me today; and in the morning I will let you go and will tell you all that is on your heart. As for your donkeys which were lost three days ago, do not set your heart on them, for they have been found. And for whom is all that is desirable in Israel? Is it not for you and for all your father's household?" And Saul answered and said, "Am I not a Benjamite, of the smallest of the tribes of Israel, and my family the least of all the families of the tribe of Benjamin? Why then do you speak to me in this way?" (1 Sam. 9:15–21)

Samuel's gift as a seer encompassed a profound discernment of the content and implications of his visions. Unlike the average observer, Samuel possessed an extraordinary sensitivity to the nuances of unfolding events. The Spirit endowed him with a keen understanding of their significance across time—past, present, and future. It seems ironic but perhaps not surprising that Samuel's insights align with the modern principles of futures studies. Like today's futurists, he weighs the implications of historical events, current pressures, and the influence of forthcoming possibilities. Unlike many in future studies, however, Samuel came to know these things through the Spirit's ways of bringing him into communion with Yahweh.

By the time we find Samuel at Zuph's city gate, he is not only advanced in age but also in wisdom and experience. He is deeply connected to the people of Israel, whom he serves with the insights that come from his continuous dialogue with Yahweh. From childhood, Samuel has been privy to divine revelations. He has guided the nation's trajectory not through book knowledge but by discerning the secrets held in the hearts of those he encounters. This spiritual insight is one of the fundamental ways Samuel understands the world around him.

The narrative in 1 Samuel 9 records a pivotal moment in Israel's history that was revealed to Samuel twenty-four hours before his encounter with Saul in Zuph. Yahweh had informed Samuel of the imminent arrival of a Benjamite man chosen to become the first king of Israel. The man was destined to lead the nation and confront the Philistines who threatened it. Samuel's anticipation of this meeting not only testifies to his prophetic gift but also to his pivotal role in the divine plan for Israel.

The text emphasizes that when Samuel meets Saul, he recognizes him in a manner that exceeds simple visual identification. Samuel perceives Saul as the one whom God had disclosed to him one day earlier.

This recognition is not superficial. Samuel sees Saul's true essence. He acknowledges the divine calling on his life, and despite the flaws that would emerge during his reign, he recognizes in him the potential and honor that are inherent in his character.

Saul was truly seen by Samuel. This profound form of recognition enabled Samuel to understand and affirm Saul's identity and potential. This act of seeing people for whom they are and can become is a rare, invaluable gift that mirrors the way God perceives us. It offers a sense of validation and inspiration that can ignite the spirit and encourage individuals to realize their divine purpose.

Today, when narcissism, pervasive insecurity, and the fear of insignificance make visibility a quality to be sought, we often misunderstand the essence of being seen. The craving for visibility obscures our ability to truly see and appreciate one another, much as the pursuit of personal recognition often overshadows our capacity for deep and empathetic connection. Vulnerabilities that were prevalent in celebrity circles have been normalized in our digital age, spreading the celebrity culture far beyond Hollywood precincts.

The story of Samuel and Saul reveals the significance of being seen in holistic ways that acknowledge our deepest potential and worth. It challenges us to look beyond superficial interactions to appreciate the unique value of every person and perceive the serendipitous moments that accompany our own lives.

Such a moment finds Saul as he searches for the seer and unknowingly approaches Samuel. We see the role of divine orchestration in Samuel's foreknowledge and Saul's unwitting manner. Samuel is already aware of Saul's coming and awaits him. Samuel then reveals himself, saying, "I am the seer." More than an act of simple self-disclosure, Samuel's statement is an unveiling of the divine intention already set in motion. It illustrates a unique way of knowing and acting in God's ways. It is a spiritual discernment anchored in divine foresight and preparation. Thus prepared, Samuel invites Saul into the revelation of divine purpose he does not yet comprehend.

As we inquire into the nuances of spiritual knowledge, the church stands at a crucial juncture. The landscape is cluttered with a mixture of authentic and misleading spiritualities that mirror our consumer-driven ethos. The church's challenge is not merely to distinguish between genuine and counterfeit expressions of spirituality but to rediscover the Spirit-led ways of knowing that have marked the church's Tradition since its inception. Then we will truly embody the Christ-centered spirituality of transformation and service.

The divine ways of knowing exemplified by Samuel's interaction with Saul are not relics of the past but essential tools for guiding the church toward a future anchored in truth. Despite the prevalence of what Eugene Peterson describes as "magic-show religion" (Gal. 5:20 MSG)—spiritual practices that entertain rather than transform[13]—the church is called to return to a spirituality by which the Spirit leads us into all truth.

This need for recovery is more than a critique. It is a call to action and re-engagement with the Holy Spirit's activity in the world. It is a call to rediscover the profound ways of knowing that can navigate the cultural complexities while staying true to the gospel's core. Such a journey requires discernment, humility, and a commitment to the transformative power of the Spirit, inviting us to see beyond the surface and to engage with the deeper realities of God's kingdom at work.

Samuel's instruction for Saul to ascend before him to the high place is both a directive and a symbolic act of leadership initiation. The moment foretells Saul's future. It is a prophetic summons that invites the possibilities of tomorrow into his present reality. A feast befitting a king awaits Saul, signifying his destiny of kingship. It is a role for which he was born but has not yet embraced. His need to recognize his calling presents a vital spiritual principle that also applies to us:

fulfilling our divine callings often requires us to rise above the malaise and spiritual apathy in which the culture is submerged.

When Kingship and Narrative Identity Clash

Ephesians 1:18–23 speaks to the royal identity in Christ that we discussed earlier. Because of it, the believer is seated with him in heavenly realms, transcending all earthly dominions (see Eph. 1:18–23). It is in conflict with the consumerist inclinations that distort this sacred calling, transposing it onto avenues of self-promotion and power imbalances, leaving many disheartened and disoriented.

Speaking for God, Samuel invited Saul to shepherd a nation in turmoil. It would require him to steer away from the societal pressures and standards of power that mirror the human race's fear-driven drive for dominance and control. Samuel presented Saul with the opportunity to embody the kingly stature Yahweh envisioned for him. The place of honor and the feast in which Saul received the most significant portion echoes the biblical motif of Benjamin before Joseph and speaks to recognition, favor, and destiny.

This exchange is ostensibly between Saul (whose name signifies desire) and Samuel (meaning, "Yahweh sees") is a moment of identity affirmation and destiny alignment. It transcends a mere meal; it will be a Eucharistic celebration where sacrifice precedes kingship. Saul will be offered the choice portion typically reserved for the priest, symbolizing his partaking in a sacrificial reality for the people's benefit. It is a transformative invitation to join a spiritual lineage, to learn to see with divine insight, and to speak with prophetic authority alongside those who dwell in the elevated realms of spiritual perception.

When Saul steps into this moment, conflict accompanies his ascent to his true purpose. He reacts to Samuel's revelation with a humility rooted in his identity as a Benjamite—a tribal history of civil strife and moral corruption that haunts Saul and makes accepting his kingship difficult. His Benjamite identification—what Dan McAdams calls "narrative identity"—is the story he and his fellow tribespeople have told themselves for generations. It now drives the unconscious realms of his mind and threatens to undermine his unexpected and serendipitous joy.[14]

Saul's inner conflict is evident in his physicality. Despite his stature, he perceives himself as lesser than other men, a view that devolves from humility to damaging self-deprecation and underscores the combination of brokenness and beauty within him—and within us. The narrative challenges us to recognize our divine callings amid the distractions of contemporary life and to embrace our places at the table prepared by divine providence, where we are invited to partake of deeper truths and engage in the redemptive missions for which we have been set apart.

To operate in the fullness of these truths and missions, healing is essential. Within secular realms and most plainly within the church, this involves a renewed vision of kingship that is epitomized by Christ's crucifixion at Golgotha, the "place of a skull." The imagery alone invites us to consider the internal battles waged within our minds. In the spaces safeguarded by our skulls, destructive narratives can dominate. They are like the thieves who desecrated the temple that Jesus cleansed in his righteous anger. His deliberative and compassionate approach was not a destructive wrath but a model for addressing the narratives that diminish our inherent worth and potential.

Crowned with thorns and crucified, Jesus embodies the ultimate paradox of kingship. He was glorified through suffering, having taken upon himself the burdens of our anxieties and iniquities for the sake of our healing and freedom. His act of sacrificial love illuminates the path from darkness to light and toward the realization of our royal callings. It is not a pursuit of earthly power but of a deeper communion with God.

In this divine narrative, we are invited to reclaim our identity as princes and princesses. We are called to a banquet of eternal significance, where we partake of Christ's self-giving love, a feast that nourishes our deepest selves and restores our narrative identity to one of hope, purpose, and divine filiation. This vision of kingship is marked by a cross that reaches to the ends of the earth and beyond. It overcomes the power of death and hostility and seeks to recover all that was lost. In this cosmic redemption, we find our true identity. We are invited to sit at the table with Christ and his Father, partaking of a life defined not by our failures but by the boundless, self-emptying love of the true King who calls us out of shadow into the unquenchable light of his presence.

Practicing Resurrection

- Both the practice of resurrection and the seizing of *kairos* moments require an openness to the Spirit's leading. Likewise, serendipity requires a heart attuned to the possibilities that lie beyond our immediate vision. Take some prayerful time to identify moments in your history when, despite your plans and regardless of any chaos, you unexpectedly bumped into important truths. How did these encounters affect your journey going forward?

- Saul knows that his quest to find the donkeys is tied to the noble qualities expressed by the first commandment to honor his parents, which is embedded deep in his core values. What are some of the cultural and ethical foundations that you uphold in good times and bad? How are they important to the culture at large?

- The distance between our vulnerability and our resilience is largely defined by how our internal narratives guide our decisions in a range of circumstances. Whether our narratives are anchored in vulnerability or resilience, our resulting self-perception influences our decision-making and the contours of our individual journeys.

How might recognizing your vulnerabilities in ways that are not inherently self-defeating foster your personal growth, empathy, and connection with others?

Notes

1. Madeline Bilis, "TBT: When the Word 'Serendipity' Was Coined," *City Life*, January 28, 2016, https://www.bostonmagazine.com/news/2016/01/28/horace-mann-serendipity/; "Horace Walpole," *Britannica*, accessed February 19, 2024, https://www.britannica.com/biography/Horace-Walpole.

2. "Horace Walpole," *Britannica*, https://www.britannica.com/biography/Horace-Walpole.

3. "Serendib," *Britannica*, accessed February 20, 2024, https://www.britannica.com/place/Serendib. Serendip (Serendib, or Ceylon) is an old Persian name for the island nation of Sri Lanka.

4. *Oxford English Dictionary*, s.v. "serendipity," accessed February 19, 2024, https://www.oed.com/dictionary/serendipity_n?tab=etymology.

5. "serendipity \-ˈdi-pə-tē\ *noun* [from its possession by the heroes of the Persian fairy tale *The Three Princes of Serendip*] 1754: the faculty or phenomenon of finding valuable or agreeable things not sought for[.] *also*: an instance of this." Merriam-Webster, *Merriam-Webster's Collegiate Dictionary* (Springfield, MA: Merriam-Webster, 2003).

6. Horace Walpole, "The Invention of Serendipity," *The Paris Review*, January 28, 2016. Horace Walpole wrote the quoted letter to Sir Horace Mann on January 28, 1754.

7. Peter Debruge, "Film Review: 'The Secret Life of Walter Mitty,'" *Variety*, October 5, 2013, https://variety.com/2013/film/markets-festivals/new-york-film-fest-review-the-secret-life-of-walter-mitty-1200698113/.

8. David Rooney, "The Secret Life of Walter Mitty: New York Film Festival Review," *Hollywood Reporter*, October 5, 2013, https://www.hollywoodreporter.com/news/general-news/secret-life-walter-mitty-new-643757/.

9. "The Secret Life of Walter Mitty (2013 Film)," Wikipedia, accessed February 19, 2024, https://en.wikipedia.org/wiki/The_Secret_Life_of_Walter_Mitty_(2013_film).

10. Castaneda, *Journey to Ixtlan*, 234.

11. Joseph Chilton Pearce, *The Crack in the Cosmic Egg* (New York: Julian Press, 1971), 7.

12. "The precondition for effectively countering the politics of fear is to challenge the association of personhood with the state of vulnerability. Anxieties about uncertainty become magnified and overwhelm us when we regard ourselves as essentially vulnerable. Yet the human imagination possesses a formidable capacity to engage and learn from the risks it faces. There is always an alternative. Whether or not we are aware of the choices confronting us depends upon whether we regard ourselves as defined by our vulnerability or by our capacity to be resilient." Kirk A. Bingaman, *Treating the New Anxiety: A Cognitive-Theological Approach* (Lanham, MD: Jason Aronson, 2007), 3.

13. "My counsel is this: Live freely, animated and motivated by God's Spirit. Then you won't feed the compulsions of selfishness. For there is a root of sinful self-interest in us that is at odds with a free spirit, just as the free spirit is incompatible with selfishness. These two ways of life are contrary to each other, so that you cannot live at times one way and at times another way according to how you feel on any given day. Why don't you choose to be led by the Spirit and so escape the erratic compulsions of a law-dominated existence. It is obvious what kind of life develops out of trying to get your own way all the time: repetitive, loveless, cheap sex; a stinking accumulation of mental and emotional garbage; frenzied and joyless grabs for happiness; trinket gods; magic-show religion; paranoid loneliness; cutthroat competition; all-consuming-yet-never-satisfied wants; a brutal temper; an impotence to love or be loved; divided homes and divided lives; small-minded and lopsided pursuits; the vicious habit of depersonalizing everyone into a rival; uncontrolled and uncontrollable addictions; ugly parodies of community. I could go on. This isn't the first time I have warned you, you know. If you use your freedom this way, you will not inherit God's kingdom" (Gal. 5:16–21 MSG).

14. Dan P. McAdams, "Narrative Identity," APA PsycNet, accessed February 19, 2024, https://psycnet.apa.org/record/2011-21882-005.

10

Honoring Your Call

In 2010, *The King's Speech* graced us with an intimate cinematic exploration of King George VI's personal struggle with a speech impediment. With his unexpected ascent to the British throne as a historical backdrop, we see Australian speech therapist Lionel Logue helping the future monarch overcome the stammer that caused him great emotional pain.

Set in the tumultuous period leading up to World War II, the story is one of personal triumph amid the pressures of leadership. *The King's Speech* is more than a historical drama; it is a narrative about a man finding his voice in the cacophony of his doubts and the weight of his nation's expectations of royalty. The story encapsulates the essence of mentorship, transformation, and the nuanced path from vulnerability to strength and from silence to eloquence. The relationship between King George VI and Logue transcends the conventional bounds of therapist and patient, evolving into a sincere friendship and foundation for the king's eventual success in uniting his country with a single, resonant voice.

Aspects of *The King's Speech* find their echo in the biblical story of Saul and his journey toward kingship. This transition, masterfully orchestrated by Yahweh and facilitated by Samuel, the seer-prophet, unfolds as an account of potential, mentorship, and divine intention. Samuel emerges as a guide and a spiritual father to the king-designate, to shepherd him into a reign defined by wisdom and righteousness.

As we know, Saul arose to the throne yet became a tragic hero. Let's explore, then, the path he might have taken by embracing his anointing and understanding the prophetic signs God bestowed on him. Let's imagine a scenario in which Saul, graced by Yahweh's spirit stirring within him, follows Samuel's wise counsel and seizes the mantle of leadership with humility and courage. In this alternate vision, Saul embodies faithfulness to the divine call, transforming his story from a diary of disappointment to a chronicle of triumph.

Samuel's anointing of Saul is a pivotal moment of affirmation and approbation. More than mere ceremony, it is a testament to Saul's potential to unite and lead Israel with integrity. Had Saul heeded the intent of Yahweh with the earnestness his call demanded, his reign could have been heralded the fulfillment of Yahweh's promises for Israel.

Saul was already in his middle years. Dr. James Hollis explains it as a period in which certain struggles arise, and the invitation to maturity comes in unexpected ways. As Dr. Hollis brilliantly explains, "We may from time to time come to realize that we are accountable for how things are playing out. When that realization occurs, a heroic summons follows: What am I asking of the other that I am not addressing myself?"[1]

When Saul is anointed as king, a heroic summons is given. What is being asked of the nation? What is being asked of others in that season? What does Saul need to address in himself? And what questions might the text be inviting *us* to consider? How might the questions asked in Saul's case invoke the transformative power of embracing our destinies with openness and faith? What about the outcomes of our own life journeys? How might our hearts be attuned to the lessons of mentorship and the various nudges, however subtle or obvious, of divine guidance?

Considered through the lens of what might have been, Saul's story mirrors our own stories and reflects the universal narrative of potential, choice, and a legacy to be defined by righteousness and faith.

A More Inspired Viewing Point

With the wisdom of years and the insight of Yahweh, Samuel invites Saul to share a meal and stay overnight. His gesture of hospitality is also an invitation into a sacred space of learning and preparation. The seer guides Saul to his chambers as the day gives way to twilight. This marks the beginning of a sacred transition, echoing the evening-and-morning rhythm from Genesis 1, in which each cycle heralds new beginnings.

As Samuel and Saul ascend to the rooftop, enveloped by the twilight's embrace, they stand on the precipice of a sacred and pivotal moment. This physically elevated space is also a more inspired viewing point, a metaphorical move above the complexities and challenges that lay below. Even in the quiet moments preceding the next morning's sacramental anointing, Israel is in turmoil, beset by conflict with the Philistines and the unsettled issue of leadership succession (1 Sam. 7:7–11).

Unlike Samuel and Saul, Israel's people have faced their trials from their less ascendant point of view: they are flat on the ground. Through Samuel's Spirit-led guidance, they have enjoyed the temporary relief of victories over the Philistines. Yet the nation's future hangs in the balance. Samuel's sons have chosen an unfortunate path, mirroring the downfall of Hophni and Phinehas. This has left Israel in a state of uncertainty and doubt. Seeking stability and a sense of hope, the elders of Israel approach Samuel and demand a king (8:4–5). Their request is not random; it surfaces amid real concerns for their collective future.

Samuel is initially troubled by the request, seeing it as a rejection of Yahweh's kingship (8:7). Yet he remembers Yahweh's promise to Jacob about kings arising from his lineage (Gen. 35:11), and he realizes that Saul's selection as king is more than a response to the people's demands; it is the fulfillment of a longstanding promise. Yahweh's decision regarding Saul's anointing is a complex interweaving of divine foresight, the people's desires, and the historic battles that have shaped their identity and aspirations. Therefore, this rooftop moment is a bridge—between Israel's past victories and future hopes of Israel, between divine promises and the people's longing for a leader they can see and touch.

As Samuel prepares Saul for the anointing at dawn, he makes Saul acutely aware of the weight of history and expectation resting on the sacred act to come. This preparation makes way for a fundamental shift in Saul's mindset. It heralds the dawn of a new era and carries the hopes of a nation yearning for stability, leadership, and a brighter future under their newly anointed king.

The rooftop refuge from the turmoil below is a powerful metaphor for our own quest for guidance, clarity, and a renewed sense of purpose in uncertain times. Just as Samuel summoned Saul to a higher purpose in that elevated sacred space, so the triune God calls us higher so we can embrace the future, despite life's lingering shadows. If we allow our sanctified imaginations to place us under the celestial dome with Samuel and Saul, we will become aware that history's pen is poised and ready to inscribe its indelible mark.

Notice that far from the clamor below, Samuel and Saul engage in a conversation meant to chart the course of a nation. According to 1 Samuel 9:25, "Samuel spoke with Saul on the roof." My sense is that Samuel is imparting something to Saul, his prophetic voice a tether between the heavenly and the earthly realms. In a moment that transcends instruction, Samuel prepares Saul's heart and soul for the responsibilities that will soon rest on him. As the first light of morning edges over the horizon, the conversation heralds Saul's emergence from obscurity to Israel's king designate. There is a sense of departure from everyday pressures and entrance into a place of insight and new beginnings. Saul glimpses a new season in which he is ordained to become a different man.

> And they got up early; and at daybreak Samuel called to Saul on the roof, saying, "Get up, so that I may send you on your way." So Saul got up, and both he and Samuel went out into the street. As they were going down to the edge of the city, Samuel said to Saul, "Speak to the servant and have him go on ahead of us and pass by; but you stand here now, so that I may proclaim the word of God to you" (9:26–27 NASB).

You can almost hear Samuel's voice, steady and purposeful as he shares the words of God with Saul. It is a rare opportunity for Saul to absorb wisdom and guidance from the prophet. This is a mentorship like no other, preparing Saul for a role that would demand not just leadership but a profound commitment to following the divine will.

Samuel gently instructs Saul, inviting him into a posture of silence and attentiveness, saying, "You stand here now, so that I may proclaim the word of God to you." This moment of quiet readiness recalls Samuel's own divine encounter as a young apprentice to Eli, which began as he lay in a state of repose near the ark of the covenant (3:1ff). Samuel had yet to experience the revelation of the Lord's word at that juncture, but this moment began his history of recognizing Yahweh's voice amid the noise and understanding that voice above all others.

When the Lord called out to Samuel, there was a familiarity and intimacy reserved for those known by name. It was the personal call of a shepherd a particular sheep, and it was later echoed in Christ's own words (John 10:27). Initially, Samuel mistook the divine summons for Eli's voice, leading him away from his sacred duties and toward Eli's resting place. Each time Samuel wrested Eli from sleep, the priest failed to discern the divine interruption and sent the boy back to his own bed. Not until the third time did the spiritually blinded Eli realize that Yahweh was calling Samuel.

In this moment, Eli offered Samuel the wisdom that would shape his response to the Lord: he told him to lie down in readiness, open to the possibility of God's voice sounding once more. He told the boy to respond by saying, "Speak, Lord, for your servant is listening" (1 Sam. 3:9 NIV).

This posture and response became a way of life for Samuel. In the twilight of his own life, Samuel seeks to impart this practice of holy listening to Saul. Samuel knows that Yahweh's voice does not emerge in the clamor of human activity but in moments of quiet openness to the divine presence. Samuel's invitation to embrace the discipline of silence is crucial for Saul. If Saul will honor it, he will hear and be transformed by the word of God.

At dawn a dramatic new chapter quietly unfolds. Saul stands on the brink of potential transformation, suspended between his past and a vast, unknown future. The voice of the venerable seer echoes with Yahweh's presence, acts as the summons, and heralds a shift in Saul's destiny and the fate of Israel. The morning marks more than Saul's anointing as king; it symbolizes a spiritual awakening to the weight and scope of true leadership.

James Hollis, reflecting on defining moments in our lives, captures the essence of this awakening: "This is what is asked of us, to show up as the person we really are, as best we can manage, under circumstances over which we may have no control. This showing up as best we can is growing up. That is all that life really asks of us: to show up as best we can."[2]

The admonition to *show up* in life points to our full engagement with our existence, which is the essence of maturity. Showing up— being present, accountable, and authentic—is what life and God demand of us. It symbolizes the transition from *being* to truly *living*. It is a process requiring us to *grow up*. In our maturation, we navigate the narrow lanes between our own actions and God's intentions. In this, guidance and active listening are critical, as are mentorship and accountability.

In considering Saul's rites of passage into kingship, may we ponder our own readiness and the influential figures who have steered us toward fulfilling our potential.

The Anointing to Reign and Rule

Then Samuel took the flask of oil, poured it on [Saul's] head, kissed him, and said, "Has not Yahweh anointed you a ruler over His inheritance?" (10:1)

Saul's anointing by Samuel is a sacramental rendezvous between the transcendent and the imminent. Anointing was already an ancient ritual in Israel; the people were well familiar with it in relation to the priesthood. Now, for the first time in Israel, it occurs in relation to kingship. Samuel, the prophet-statesman, stands before Saul, flask in hand, and is acting on behalf of Yahweh. He performs an act intended to irrevocably alter the course of Saul's life and Israel's. Samuel pours the fragrant oil on Saul's head as a tangible representation of Yahweh's Spirit descending and marking Saul with a sacred purpose.

For Saul, the uniqueness of the oil's fragrance and the sensation of it cascading down his head could provoke a visceral awareness of being set apart by Yahweh for a task of monumental importance. Of this we cannot be certain, yet the intent is not in doubt. This moment is designed to transcend the physical. In it, Saul's joy in being selected by God mingles with the weight of the responsibility he now bears. As feelings of awe and humility perhaps wash over him, so too does a nascent sense of the burden of kingship.

Then comes the kiss—a simple gesture of endorsement and affection from Samuel. This isn't a mere sign of respect but an intimate affirmation of Saul's new role and identity. In the context of their shared culture, the kiss seals a covenant, binding Samuel and Saul in a relationship marked by loyalty, protection, and divine purpose. It would seem intended for Saul to feel a surge of validation and encouragement, a warm reassurance that he does not step into this calling alone but with the support and favor of both Samuel and God.

In Samuel's evocative inquiry—"Has not Yahweh anointed you a ruler over His inheritance?"—a rich dimension of the anointing ceremony is revealed. The question affirms that Yahweh is orchestrating events through Samuel's actions. The act of anointing Saul transcends the matter of appointment and signifies a sacred trust being established for the welfare of God's people. Samuel's query emphasizes that Saul's role encompasses not only leadership but a stewardship of great magnitude.

As Saul contemplates Samuel's question, his internal turmoil implies his struggle with the enormity of the responsibility being bestowed on him. I cannot help but wonder how the course of history might have been altered had Saul been openhearted rather than apprehensive. Saul was correct in gauging the responsibility to be great. The anointing itself symbolized the weightiness of covenant—not only between the leader and the people, but between the leader and God.

Saul's realization provokes our own reflection on the implications of accepting the divine call with humility and courage. The lesson for Saul is a foundational precedent for all who are called to lead. It's an invitation for each of us to consider the divine summons for which we are accountable. Each of us is anointed and appointed by God for purposes that transcend our understanding. Saul's story reminds us that grace underpins our callings, and courage is required to embrace it. Our narrative identity changes in such moments, as Saul's did. A journey of discernment, faith, and personal transformation beckons us to see beyond the surface and step into our God-given destiny with open hearts and willing spirits.

The Oil and Flask

The narrative describing Saul's anointing for kingship is brimming with symbols. In some cases, the imagery relates physical acts and articles with divine realities, while other details remind us of the paradox of Christ living within human vessels.

The Work of the Apothecary

In Exodus 30:22–25, we find details for the creation of the holy anointing oil, which is described as the "work of the apothecary" (KJV). More than a list of ingredients, this divine recipe suggests a spiritual and sacramental reality to which each spice and component contributes. The apothecary's work prepares a substance that symbolizes the consecration and sanctification of God's chosen servants. The oil is a careful blend of myrrh, cinnamon, cane (calamus), cassia, and olive oil—each element carrying its own symbolic weight. The bitter fragrance of myrrh symbolizes the bitterness of sacrifice but also the sweetness of resurrection and life, which points to the death and resurrection of Christ. The warm aroma of cinnamon represents the zeal and fervor of the Spirit; cane (calamus) symbolizes righteousness and purity; cassia and its low-growing nature bring humility to mind; and olive oil, the base of the mixture, symbolizes the anointing of the Holy Spirit, who provides light, healing, and nourishment.

The meticulous preparation of the anointing oil embodies the essence of God's instructions to Moses. The precise blending of ingredients also creates a substance imbued with the power to consecrate and set apart objects and individuals for sacred service. The anointing oil thus becomes a tangible manifestation of God's presence and blessing, marking the anointed as holy and separated unto God. This sacramental nature of the anointing points to the interconnectedness of the physical and spiritual realms in the worship practices of ancient Israel. It was used in physical acts—the anointing of priests, kings, and sacred objects—through which spiritual realities were acknowledged and celebrated. Use of the sacred oil confirmed encounter with the divine; it was a sacramental expression of being chosen, sanctified, and empowered by God's Spirit.

The Ceramic Flask

"Samuel took the flask of oil, poured it on [Saul's] head, kissed him, and said, 'Has not Yahweh anointed you a ruler over His inheritance?'" (1 Sam. 10:1). Notice that the oil was in a ceramic flask, a small jug.[3] This receptacle has a distinct symbolic significance. Being a material crafted from the earth and then fired and hardened implies a panoply of meanings within the context of sacred anointing. The material from clay echoes the Genesis imagery of humanity itself being fashioned from the earth (Gen. 2:7). Paralleling the creation of the vessel and the creation of humanity suggests a connection to the divine Potter, who shapes and forms both the vessel and its anointed recipient according to his purpose. The shaping, molding, and firing processes used in creating ceramic mirrors the spiritual formation and testing that prepare individuals for divine service.

Because ceramics are transformed and hardened by fire, they emerge as vessels of purity and sanctification, capable of holding sacred anointing oil without contaminating it. This separation from impurity mirrors the anointing's intent to consecrate and dedicate a human vessel for divine service. The choice of a ceramic flask highlights the transformative sanctification process we, too, undergo when set apart for a divine calling. The humble yet potent flask embodies our own role as vessels of God's Spirit. Just as the flask carries and dispenses the anointing oil, we are called to bear and share the grace and gifts of the Holy Spirit. This parallel draws us closer to the heart of our purpose, reminding us that we are instruments through whom God's will is realized; we are channels of his presence and power in the world.

The ceramic flask in Saul's anointing invites us to consider the depth and sanctity of our own callings. The vessel's significance—marked by divine craftsmanship, an enduring covenant, and a commitment to purity and service—deepens our understanding of what it means to be chosen and set apart for God's purposes. It is a reminder of the sacred responsibility and honor that accompany our anointing and empowerment by the Holy Spirit.

The inherent balance between a ceramic jug's durability and fragility speaks to our human condition. While such vessels can preserve their contents for extended periods, they remain vulnerable to breakage. This duality resonates with our own experiences of brokenness and beauty as we move toward wholeness and completion. It suggests that, despite our fragility, we hold within us a treasure of immense value—the light and life of the Spirit in jars of clay, a testament to God's power made perfect in our imperfections.

We have this treasure in jars of clay, to show that the surpassing power belongs to God and not to us. We are afflicted in every

way, but not crushed; perplexed, but not driven to despair; persecuted, but not forsaken; struck down, but not destroyed; always
carrying in the body the death of Jesus, so that the life of Jesus
may also be manifested in our bodies. For we who live are always
being given over to death for Jesus' sake, so that the life of Jesus
also may be manifested in our mortal flesh. So death is at work
in us, but life in you.

Since we have the same spirit of faith according to what has
been written, "I believed, and so I spoke," we also believe, and
so we also speak, knowing that he who raised the Lord Jesus will
raise us also with Jesus and bring us with you into his presence.
(2 Cor. 4:7–14 ESV).

Paul's experience, embodied in the metaphor of "treasure in jars
of clay," speaks directly to our hearts and reveals the truth of God's
power shining through our everyday weaknesses. The challenges and
suffering Paul encountered on his own path were inseparable from his
dedication to sharing the gospel. His experience is a vivid example of
how God's extraordinary strength shines through our fragility.

Saul and Paul

Remember, it was Saul of Tarsus who became Paul the apostle. Named
by his father after Israel's first king, Saul's name signified a legacy
filled with honor and hopes of greatness. Yet, Saul of Tarsus was ultimately given the name *Paul* (which means "small"). This name-change
reminds us that our backgrounds, names, and pasts are engrained
in our callings. When the apostle to the Gentiles described his life-
changing encounter on the road to Damascus, he said that Jesus called
him by his birth name, saying, "Saul, Saul, why are you persecuting
Me?" (Acts 9:4). This moment connected Saul's future mission with
his roots, bridging the gap between his presumed call and his divine

call. The community recognized his transformation by calling him Paul, but it was about more than a new name; in changing his name, they acknowledged his changed life and his new role as messenger to the Gentiles.

This beautiful interplay between Saul's heritage, his encounter with Christ, and his role in the early church can inspire all of us. It shows that our past, with all its complexities, is not discarded by God but integrated into our individual and collective callings. Like Saul who became known as Paul, we are all on a journey where our identity (shaped by our history, encounters with God, and the recognition of our community) plays a crucial role in how we relate to our calling in God. The story of Saul of Tarsus remind us that our weaknesses are the very places where God's power shines brightest, and our pasts, no matter how complicated, are part of the grand design that the Eternal God has for each of us.

Like Paul, we are called to embrace our entire story, with our trials, transformations, and triumphs as integral pieces of God's masterpiece. When Paul mentions a "treasure," he's opening our hearts to the breathtaking reality of the Holy Spirit living within us. Imagine! Within our everyday selves resides the promise of "Christ in you, the hope of glory" (Col. 1:27). This isn't an offhand or lofty idea; it is the Spirit actively working in us, shaping us for a glorious future we can only begin to comprehend.

Ephesians 1:14 paints this beautifully, describing the Spirit as our "earnest" or down payment, a guarantee of the incredible inheritance that awaits us. Paul is encouraging us to contemplate the paradox inherent in our Christian identity: we are mere clay vessels, yet we contain a divine treasure. This juxtaposition does not spotlight our failings; it celebrates God's grace, which is magnified through our flaws and leads us toward glorification. Ben Witherington III enriches our understanding by suggesting that the choice of earthen vessels (perhaps akin to the fragile yet light-emitting pottery lamps of Corinth) symbolizes how our very fragility can amplify the light of Christ within us.[4]

By embracing our role as humble carriers of this heavenly treasure, we are invited to reflect the self-emptying (kenotic) love of Christ that illuminates a path of grace transcending our earthly limitations. This idea draws a contrast between the treasure contained within us and the vessel itself. Our own fragility can paradoxically serve to emit more of the divine light we carry within. This is not unlike Jesus's declaration that he is the vine and we are the branches (John 15:1–5). Just as branches derive their life and ability to bear fruit from the vine, we also draw our strength and purpose from Christ, the indwelling Spirit that is our treasure.

Our worth and capacity to illuminate the world with the light of Christ are not predicated on our inherent qualities but on the Christ of glory within us. The commonplace, fragile pottery, when filled with oil and lit, transforms into a source of light, guiding steps in the darkness. Similarly, we, though fragile and unremarkable in ourselves, become bearers of the Christ's light, guiding others not by our strength but by the light of Jesus within us.

Shadows and Sunlight

Following his mention of "jars of clay" in 2 Corinthians 4, Paul outlines a series of paradoxes that we experience; we are "afflicted, but not crushed; perplexed, but not despairing; persecuted but not forsaken; struck down, but not destroyed" (2 Cor. 4:8–9). Paul is articulating the tension between his human frailty and the resilience granted to him (and us) by the indwelling Spirit. Witherington notes that Paul's use of language, particularly in expressing his trials through pairs of apparent contradictions, underscores Paul's deep trust in God's sovereignty and redemptive power. His declaration of being "perplexed but not despairing" testifies of this trust and denotes a resilience and king-ship not of this world but rooted in the wisdom and strength of God. Paul's experiences, marked by both suffering and divine victory, echo the paradoxical nature of Christ's own kingship, which is exemplified through service, sacrifice, and, ultimately, triumph over death.

Paul is telling us that we are walking a path marked by both shad-ows and sunlight, where moments of struggle are intertwined with moments of triumph. The essence of the Jesus journey is that Jesus is the way; he is the journey (John 14:7).

Paul is letting us know in vivid, transparent language what he experientially *knew* of crucifixion and resurrection in his daily walk. If the pattern sounds distant, it remains incredibly close in our lives. Think about the times when you face challenges that seem insur-mountable. The weight of the world presses down on you and makes every step feel like a march through quicksand. Paul knew this feeling well. He faced intense afflictions, yet they never had the final say.

Like him, you have felt bewildered by life's complexities, finding yourself at various crossroads and shrouded in fog. Yet somehow, a path has always emerged; an inner witness of the Spirit has illumi-nated a way forward. Sometimes, you experienced what Pentecostals are inclined to call a "quickening." One way or another, however, you cleared the crossroads and exited the fog.

All of us have been abandoned in some way. Paul was no stranger to the sting of rejection. Like us, he received the cold shoulder for his embrace of Christ and the cruciform life. He felt isolated, targeted, and sometimes left to stand alone against the tide. Every follower of Christ has similar war stories. But Paul realized that he was never truly abandoned. The Lord was his constant companion, providing strength when his own ebbed away.

Yes, there were times when the blows life dealt Paul felt utterly crushing, as if the very ground beneath his feet might give way. He experienced the very depths of despair (2 Cor. 1:8–10), moments when it seemed the end was near. Yet death never had the last word. The expression "perplexed, but not driven to despair" might seem to contradict Paul's admission in 2 Corinthians 1:8–9 of being burdened beyond his strength, to the point of despairing of life itself. Perhaps the key to the seeming clash lies in understanding the context and the depth of Paul's trust in God. In his moment of utmost vulnerability, he reaches a climactic realization: his experience of despair, of feeling the "sentence of death" within, serves a divine purpose—to shift his (and his apostolic team's) reliance away from his (their) own strength and toward God, who raises the dead.

The seeming contradiction is in fact a profound lesson in the dynamics of faith. Paul is illuminating the process of coming to trust in God's power to bring life from death and thereby *to practice resurrection*. The despair he experienced was not the end but a means to deepen his reliance on God. It taught him and his companions to see beyond their immediate circumstances to the God who delivers and who transforms situations of utter hopelessness into testimonies of his power to save and renew.

Through every trial, every tear, every heartache, there was always a flicker of life, a whisper of resurrection promise. This pattern of dying and rising isn't Paul's story alone. It is yours. In every hardship, a hidden seed of renewal and hope is also present. Your walk with Jesus is replete with such paradoxes. Moments of crucifixion are always followed by resurrection. In the gritty reality of walking by faith and not sight, the trials of affliction, the maze of perplexity, the heat of persecution, and even the chill of death's shadow are but chapters. They are intense and sometimes nearly insurmountable, yet they are not the entirety of your story. They set the stage for the transformative power of resurrection life, a promise that dawn's light follows the darkest night.

These words will never diminish the reality of pain. They are not offered as trite consolation. They are about recognizing the profound truth that in every struggle, there's a hidden river of divine grace leading us toward a place of renewal that only faith can see.

Consider Paul's assertion in Romans 5:17: "For if by the offense of the one, death reigned through the one, much more will those who receive the abundance of grace and of the gift of righteousness reign in life through the One, Jesus Christ." Paul's life exemplifies reigning in life through the grace and righteousness provided by Christ Jesus.

This reigning is not characterized by earthly power or dominion but by living in the victory and authority of the resurrected Christ. It is here, in the wisdom of God and the power of redemption, that Saul of Tarsus becomes what King Saul could not. Through his faith and apostolic calling, Paul demonstrates what it means to truly reign in life—not by wielding power over others but by manifesting the life of Jesus in every circumstance. This is what leads to the reign characterized by grace, redemption, and eternal hope.

Paul's words about "always carrying in the body the death of Jesus" are not theological jargon. They touch on something deeply personal for each of us. It involves stepping into the very footsteps of Christ, embracing our own moments of suffering as avenues to resurrection life. It's about a journey of transfiguration, that of necessity, starts from within. It is a moment-by-moment letting go of self-centeredness and the ways in which the principle of sin that is at work in "the law of sin and death" seeks to undermine our progress (Rom. 8:2). Instead, we are to prove what is good, agreeable, and mature—the will of God that reveals itself in honorable sonship and daughterhood (Rom. 12:1–3). Each day we are summoned to offer ourselves up as living sacrifices, presenting our total personhood—heart, mind, and body—to the One who called us out of darkness into his marvelous light. It's in this very act of giving ourselves over to "death for Jesus' sake" that we find true life sprouting within us, even in our mortal, flawed bodies.

Paul goes further, suggesting that this journey through death not only transforms us; it somehow brings life to others too. This mysterious exchange, in which our sacrifices and sufferings can result in blessings and new beginnings for those around us, mirrors the very heart of Christ's ministry. Through our lives, the Spirit of life that raised Jesus from the dead flows out (8:2), touching and transforming those we encounter. This cycle of dying and rising with Christ isn't just a one-time event; it's the very rhythm of Christian living. It reflects Jesus's own journey from death to resurrection, reminding us that our path is marked by the same pattern. It is a challenging, sometimes painful journey, but it's also filled with hope, promise, and the incredible potential to see ourselves and others brought into the fullness of life in Christ.

One final thought: When we truly believe in something that grips our heart and soul, we are compelled to speak about it and share it with the world. When we are so deeply moved by something in life that affects our understanding in earth-shattering ways (and what could be more earth-shattering than an encounter with the risen and ascended Christ?), how can you not do what Saul did? He was struck down from a galloping steed at noonday on the road to Damascus. So radical was his experience that it took him three days to resume the usual routine of existence. Is it any wonder than when he was finally apprehended by Jesus that he fervently traversed cities and towns? It was not out of a sense of duty; it was because he was impelled forward by an unshakeable conviction in the abiding presence of the ascended Christ with his people, his church.

There was nothing casual about the way Paul spoke after his initial encounter with Christ. His entire way of seeing changed, which altered his way of perceiving what he was seeing and observing. This in turn altered his way of interpreting his perceptions, which changed his way of speaking. When faith speaks, what is spoken is brought to speech under the all-pervasive thrust of the indwelling Spirit of faith himself.

The Spirit, who indwelt Paul, indwells you and me. He is the very Spirit who works in time and yet transcends it. This reminds us that God's Spirit has been at work in the hearts of the faithful across the ages, nurturing a deep-seated belief and a readiness to proclaim his great love.

Practicing Resurrection

- How might God be calling you to a "rooftop refuge" in your quest for guidance, clarity, and a renewed sense of purpose? What "facts on the ground" tend to keep you from such elevated sacred spaces? Explain.

- Assuming that Yahweh's voice does not emerge in the clamor of human activity but becomes evident in our moments of quiet openness to the divine presence, how might the discipline of silence benefit you in this season? How will you honor it?

- Considering the ceramic flask in Saul's anointing as a symbol of the depth and sanctity of your own calling, how do its qualities correspond to or differ from yours?

Notes

1. James Hollis, *Living an Examined Life: Wisdom for the Second Half of the Journey* (Louisville, CO: Sounds True, 2018), 17.

2. Hollis, *Living an Examined Life*, 18.

3. "פַךְ,'flask, vial, phial, i.e., a small jug as a container to hold liquid (1Sa 10:1; 2Ki 9:1, 3+)." James Swanson, *Dictionary of Biblical Languages with*

Semantic Domains: Hebrew (Old Testament) (Oak Harbor, WA: Logos Research Systems, 1997), s.v. "פַּךְ."

4. Ben Witherington III, *Conflict and Community in Corinth: A Socio-Rhetorical Commentary on 1 and 2 Corinthians* (Grand Rapids, MI: Eerdmans, 1995), 386–87.

Allowing the Spirit to Lead

The Matrix.[1] Released just at the dawn of the new millennium (1999), this groundbreaking film directed by the Wachowskis offers a dystopian vision of a future where humanity is unknowingly trapped in a simulated reality, controlled by machines. It's a world where the true nature of things is hidden beneath layers of illusion, and liberation requires awakening to a deeper truth. The protagonist, Thomas Anderson, known by his hacker alias *Neo*, finds himself questioning the nature of his reality. Guided by the enigmatic Morpheus and the formidable Trinity, Neo is awakened to the truth of the Matrix and his role in the fight against the oppressors of humanity. His journey from an ordinary software engineer to the prophesied "One" is not just a tale of heroism but an elaborate allegory of awakening, transformation, and redemption.

Far more than a high-octane blend of science fiction and action, the film is a philosophical inquiry into freedom, reality, and the power of belief. It challenges us to question the constructs that define our world and to consider the potential within us to transcend those boundaries. With its rich symbolism and narrative depth, *The Matrix* serves as a compelling entry point into our final consideration of aspects of Saul's journey to the throne of Israel, the mentorship of Samuel, and the consciousness-expanding power of facing our own shadows. As we stand at the threshold of the three signs that come upon Saul after he is anointed as king-designate by Samuel, it is not all that hard to think of Thomas Anderson-become-Neo as he enters the matrix. Like Saul, Neo begins his journey in obscurity, unaware of the full extent of his potential or the pivotal role he's destined to play in the liberation of humanity. Guided by the wise Morpheus, the mentor who sees beyond the facade of the virtual world to the deeper reality beneath, Neo is led through a series of revelations and trials that ultimately prepare him for his role as a leader and liberator. The flow of the plot not only mirrors Saul's anointing and the guidance he receives from Samuel; it also resonates with our own journey through the cultural and spiritual upheavals of our time.

Neo's journey is marked by three kairotic moments that awaken him to his true identity and mission. So, too, three signs foretold by Samuel are intended to be transforming moments, perhaps even "eureka moments" and not merely plot points. For Neo, his three moments are encounters that challenge him to see beyond his current reality, to embrace his potential, and to step into his destined role. They serve as a metaphor for our own need to navigate the complexities of our era with adaptive resilience and radical hope, guided by mentors who help us see the world, and our place in it, with newfound clarity. If we give careful consideration to the signs that marked Saul's path to kingship, we realize the importance of those mentors in our lives who have acted or are currently acting as our own "Morpheuses," or perhaps reveal to us our need for mentors and knowing where to find them. Knowing where to find those who embody a wisdom that is timeless—and yet understand the times, past, present, and future—and can impart that wisdom to us so that we can know what to do to move forward with at least some sense of confidence that our steps are being ordered by God. Somewhere in the uncertainty, we need the rebuilding of a confidence that our spiritual sight is being perfected and that we are seeing things more clearly and comprehending the reason we find ourselves where we are at this juncture of history, rightly honoring the weight of the past, owning the pressure of the present, and experiencing the powerful pull of the future.

In our journey, we often wonder about finding the right mentors— those wise souls who can guide us through life's complexities. I am persuaded deeply of the serendipitous hand of Providence in these matters. It's not merely about our seeking out these mentors; rather, it's about being open to the One who orders our steps on the appropriate path at just the right moments. It is a divine partnership, where our heartfelt longing to grow and learn is met with God's gracious provision of people who can lead us through unlearning, relearning, and new learning. This "dance" between our efforts and God's providence reminds us that we're never alone in our quest. God, in infinite wisdom, connects us with those who help us navigate life's liminal spaces with courage and purpose, honoring the past while boldly stepping into the future. Ours is to remain open and trusting, for the right mentors, those precious seers like Samuel, are indeed a gift from above, perfectly timed to enrich our lives and deepen our journey with God.

Mentors and the Pull of the Future

The Greeks, whose philosophical and educational systems have profoundly influenced Western civilization, placed great emphasis on the mentor-mentee relationship. The very term *mentor* originates from Homer's *Odyssey*,[2] in which the character Mentor is entrusted with the education of Telemachus, son of Odysseus. This relationship was characterized by guidance, knowledge transfer, and moral and social education, laying a foundation for the individual's development and integration into society.[3]

"The word mentor calls to mind the Greek word *meno*, meaning 'to abide' or 'to remain.' The mentoring context frequently involves an intimate, committed, continuous, developmental, and reciprocal relationship. This relationship includes a reciprocal availability, where unforced influence and helpfulness take place."[4] These words from Dean Thompson and D. Cameron Murchison are saying that mentoring is about abiding together in a journey of growth and discovery—a journey marked by an intimate, committed, and continuous relationship. This isn't merely an exchange of knowledge or skills but a shared path where both mentor and mentee remain open to learning from each other, fostering a developmental and reciprocal bond. "Unforced influence" seems to imply that the influence flows naturally, where help and guidance are offered without coercion and where both individuals are available to each other in a manner that's as natural as it is profound. This kind of mentoring brings to light the essence of human connection—where we are not just teachers or learners but partners in the unfolding story of our lives. A mentor is not just a guide; rather the mentor is a guardian of potential, a cultivator of wisdom, and a model of virtue. True mentoring is an art that nurtures the whole person, fostering intellectual growth, character development, and potential realization. It's about creating a supportive space for exploration, questioning, and discovering one's place in the world, guided by someone who truly cares for their mentee's total well-being.

Mentoring is a reciprocal exchange, a balance of giving and taking that enriches both mentor and mentee. It's about presence, support, and mutual growth, transcending roles to foster continuous learning. This relationship encourages us to engage with each other openly, embracing the journey of growth with humility and commitment. In essence, mentoring is a way of life that honors our interconnected journeys and our collective pursuit of wisdom and fulfillment.

At the same time, Thomson and Murchison quote David Brooks and his work on mentoring, *The Road to Character*, in which he says, "We all need people to tell us when we are wrong, to advise us on how to do right, and to encourage, support, arouse, cooperate and inspire us along the way."[5]

Mentorship therefore involves triumphs, corrections, and essential guidance rooted in deep care and wisdom. It's a journey enriched by mentors who offer both applause and candid counsel, echoing the proverb "iron sharpens iron" (Prov. 27:17) to refine us. This relationship extends beyond the present, allowing us to draw wisdom from those long past through their writings, shaping our thoughts and actions across time. The Scriptures are not merely a collection of historical records and spiritual teachings; they are a living, breathing source of mentorship. The simple reason for this? The Scriptures are "God-breathed" (2 Tim. 3:16). Through the inspiration of the Holy Spirit, the experiences and teachings of the figures in the narratives of Scripture become more than historical anecdotes; they become living words that speak directly to our hearts and circumstances. In this way, "the communion of the saints" spoken of in the Apostle's Creed—in the third article of the creed, which is about the role of the Spirit in the economy of salvation—becomes a dynamic interaction where the wisdom of the past illuminates our present and guides our future. The figures we encounter in its stories—from the patriarchs and prophets to the apostles and martyrs—all have something to teach us. Their lives, marked by faith, struggle, triumph, and sometimes failure, offer us a rich tapestry of lessons on how to navigate the complexities of life with integrity, courage, and faith. To engage with the words of these spiritual mentors through contemplation and meditation on the sacred text encourages us to reflect on our own lives, to question, to seek, and to grow. This process of learning and growth is not a solitary journey but a communal voyage, enriched by the voices of those who have journeyed before us.

From Moses guiding Joshua to prepare him for leadership after his departure, to Deborah's pivotal role in empowering Barak, these stories highlight the critical role of mentorship in facilitating significant, sometimes seismic, shifts in personal and communal trajectories. Naomi's tender yet strategic mentoring of Ruth not only secures their mutual survival but also ensures Ruth's place in the lineage of David and, ultimately, Jesus Christ. Similarly, the story of Queen Esther reveals an unconventional form of mentorship, where her influence over King Xerxes and her bold actions mentor a whole nation in courage and faith. The mentoring relationship between Elijah and Elisha further exemplifies the passage of spiritual mantle and wisdom, demonstrating the depth of change that mentorship can instigate.

In the New Testament, the mentoring dynamics continue to reveal deep insights into the nature of deep change and growth. Mary and Elizabeth's relationship, for example, showcases mutual mentorship rooted in faith and shared experience, offering profound lessons in navigating divine callings. Similarly, Jesus's relationship with his disciples stands as the quintessential model of mentorship, guiding them from uncertainty to a place of profound understanding and purpose.

The mentoring of Apollos by Priscilla (far more than Aquila) highlights the importance of theological and spiritual mentorship within the early Christian community, underscoring the value of knowledge and wisdom in faith's journey. Paul and Timothy, along with Barnabas and John Mark, further illustrate how mentorship in the Christian context is about nurturing faith, character, and ministry. These examples from Scripture, spanning from the ancient paths of Israel to the early church's burgeoning communities, underscore a vital conviction:

the journey to realizing our potential is intricately woven with the guidance and support of mentors. Through their wisdom, challenges, and shared experiences, mentors help us navigate the complexities of our callings and the uncertainties of growth.

As we turn our attention now to the first sign that Samuel predicts Saul will encounter after their parting—a sign that will confirm the divine anointment and set the stage for his future leadership—we are reminded of the influence that mentorship congruent with divine guidance can have on our path to the future. What Samuel reveals to Saul invites us to reflect on the ways in which guidance and signs in our own lives can lead to deep change.

Rachel's Tomb

When you go from me today, then you will find two men close to Rachel's tomb in the territory of Benjamin at Zelzah; and they will say to you, "The donkeys which you went to search for have been found. Now behold, your father has ceased to be concerned about the donkeys and is anxious for you, saying, 'What shall I do about my son?'" (1 Sam. 10:2)

Listening carefully to Samuel's words is more than a historical recount; it's an invitation to engage with our own "signs" in a way that makes room for us to actually ask questions of our mentors. At the very least, it is prompting us to ask ourselves, Are we truly listening to Samuel's enduring wisdom as it relates to how we apply this in our walk with Christ?

Samuel, though long since departed, is inspiring us to seek, recognize, and embrace the guidance that is offered to us here in the text, ensuring we learn what it means to reign and rule in life in the era in which we are called to bear witness to the One who sits enthroned as

King of kings and Lord of lords. I would suggest that there are *three essential insights* that we need to pay attention to in regard to genuine prophetic insight and foresight:

1. *Prophetic hindsight and insight are invaluable:* Samuel *sees* that the formerly lost donkeys are presently found. It's a vivid reminder of how genuine mentorship connects us to where we have been and where we are now. It never seeks to identify current reality apart from how we got "here." There is a "where" we started that always has to be honored and acknowledged.

2. *Prophetic clarity includes a seeing heart:* There's a shift—from lost donkeys to a father's worry, from a quest for animals to the deep concern for a son. This pivot isn't just about changing subjects; it's about understanding our actions' ripple effects, recognizing that our personal quests have deeper implications for those we love. It's a lesson in seeing beyond our immediate concerns to the hearts of those around us.

3. *Prophetic revelation never ignores the significance of death:* The prophetic sign leads us directly to Rachel's tomb, a site imbued with layers of history and profound symbolism. This place isn't merely a geographical marker; it serves as spiritual geography in the territory of the human heart—your heart and my heart and where they intersect with the God who has placed eternity in our hearts (Eccles. 3:11). Standing at this juncture of memory and mourning, we are gently reminded that our paths are woven into a vast tapestry of faith and perseverance. Rachel's death and burial "on the way" (Gen. 35:19–20) to Bethlehem, culminating in her giving life as she herself steps into death, hints at the Christocentric act of self-sacrificial, self-emptying love.

The very existence of the tribe of Benjamin springs from this act of love—a love between Rachel and Jacob, a love that gave him first Joseph after twenty-one years of enduring the dark night of barrenness, and then Benjamin, a testament to life birthed through sacrifice. Moreover, Rachel's resting place on the route to Bethlehem, the destined birthplace of the Messiah, underscores her death's prophetic role within the expansive saga of redemption. Through this, Samuel subtly beckons Saul to acknowledge that the journey toward God's envisioned future for us often requires a deep understanding that our victories, our overcoming of adversities, are intricately tied to the essence of sacrificial love, as encapsulated in Revelation 12:11: "And they overcame him because of the blood of the Lamb and because of the word of their witness, and they did not love their life even to death." Herein lies the invitation to grasp that true overcoming is rooted not in the avoidance of our trials but in a profound comprehension of sacrifice and witness.

Rachel's tomb is also a prophetic reminder to both those exiled to Babylon and the returnees, seventy years later, as they made their journey back to the land of promise. This sacred site, a symbol of both loss and hope, was a beacon that they passed, connecting their present struggles and aspirations with the deep roots of their ancestral past. For the exiles, Rachel's tomb may have evoked feelings of sorrow and displacement, reminiscent of Rachel's own tears for her children, yet it also stood as a testament to the enduring strength and resilience of their faith. Upon their return, this same tomb underscored the fulfillment of promise and the cyclical nature of redemption and renewal. In this way, Rachel's tomb transcended its role as a mere physical landmark; it became a spiritual touchstone for the people of Israel, reminding them of their journey through despair and toward hope, guided by the legacy of faith that sustained them through their darkest times and back into the light of their promised future.

Moreover, it is Rachel's weeping that is "heard" in Israel, when her name is invoked in the slaughter of the innocents under Herod the Great. As Herod's brutal decree unfolds in the shadows of Jesus's birth in Bethlehem, Scripture draws us back to Rachel, symbolizing her as weeping for her children, the young lives extinguished in Herod's holocaust. This reference, deeply embedded in the collective memory of a people familiar with suffering and loss, bridges the gap between the ancient sorrow at Rachel's tomb and the new agony encountered at the advent of the Messiah. Her tears, transcending time, become a universal lament for all children lost to the violence of power, connecting the historical pain of exile and return with the grief experienced at the dawn of Christ's kingdom. In this way, Rachel's legacy is not only one of life and sacrifice but also of enduring maternal grief, echoing through the ages as a reminder of the cost of redemption and the depth of a love that mourns deeply for the lost. Rachel's cries give voice to trauma, pain, and horror of Israel's sufferings. They need a voice. Rachel is that prophetic voice of mourning. It is a weeping and a travail that moves the salvation history of God forward to the splitting open of heaven at the baptism of Jesus in the Jordan when God breaks the seeming silence and affirms the Incarnate Elect Son as the fullness of Israel's hopes and promises. Herod attempted to eliminate Mary's Boy Child, yet like the donkeys that evaded Saul's grasp, the powers of darkness were no match for the God who hid Christ in such a way that the devil did not know where he was even though they sent an entourage to Bethlehem. God was and is always one step (at the very least) ahead of the powers.

The paradox at the heart of the Christian faith is that through suffering and death comes new life and redemption. This cycle of mourning turning to joy, of death giving way to resurrection, is central to our story and our identity as the sons and daughters of God. Rachel's tears serve not only as a memorial to grief and loss but also as a testament to the enduring promise of restoration and renewal. In the shadow of Christ's resurrection, her legacy invites Saul and us to hold fast to the belief that out of the deepest despair can come the greatest renewal, embodying the practice of resurrection as a living hope that transforms sorrow into joy and death into a new beginning.

The Oak of Tabor

> Then you will go on further from there, and you will come as far as the oak of Tabor, and there three men going up to God at Bethel will meet you, one carrying three young goats, another carrying three loaves of bread, and another carrying a jug of wine; and they will greet you and give you two loaves of bread. And you will take them from their hand (1 Sam. 10:3–4).

Throughout the Near East from ancient times (of the many hundreds of species of oak trees globally), the Palestinian oaks are found in higher elevations, and Tabor oaks flourish at lower altitudes.[6] Susan Rattray tells us that the oak symbolizes strength.[7] It is at the Tabor oaks of Mamre that Abraham builds an altar to the Lord and worships (Gen. 13:18). Israel committed idolatry under oak trees by offering sacrifices to pagan gods (Hos. 4:13). Oaks are sign of the longevity that endures past judgment and will burn with the fires of renewal long after the devastation passes (Isa. 6:13). It was under the boughs of the oak at Mamre (Gen. 18:1–5) where Abraham hosted divine visitors and God announced the birth of Isaac. The oak is a site of weeping, when and where Rebekah's nurse, Deborah, was laid to rest (35:8). It was an oak under which Deborah, the prophetess, dispensed justice. Isaiah speaks of the saints as "oaks of righteousness, the planting of the Lord" (Isa. 61:3), envisioning a people transformed by God's grace, standing tall in the face of adversity, a living testament to divine glory.

As Saul comes to the oak of Tabor, that oak stands in solidarity as a witness to a salvation history from the hand of Yahweh that is rooted in the past, growing in the present, and reaching toward the future.

There at the oak, three men ascending to the historic site of Bethel (the gate of heaven, the house of God) to worship the God of Israel give Saul bread yet not wine. To be given bread was an indication of Saul being "privileged to receive priestly portions."[8] Yet they do not give him wine. As Peter Leithart notes, "Bread is the food of beginnings, giving strength to the heart of man (Ps. 104:15). But wine is to gladden the heart and comes at the end, when the work is done."[9]

Saul's receipt of two of the three loaves of bread underscores his participation in the priestly portion. Leithart tells us, "Though Saul became king, in an important sense the Israelite king was also a prophetic and priestly figure."[10]

Saul's encounter with the provision of bread, in the absence of wine, subtly prefigures the comprehensive redemption found in Christ, the Bread of Life (John 6:51), whose sacrifice nourishes the world. This episode, while highlighting Saul's immediate sustenance, also points toward a greater spiritual feast: the Eucharist. Here, Jesus offers both bread, symbolizing his body, and wine, representing his blood, thus inaugurating a new and everlasting covenant. This sacred meal transcends the temporary and partial covenants of the past, including Saul's kingship, embodying God's ultimate act of salvation. This moment therefore is a sign that invites us to anticipate the Eucharist, where the fullness of God's promise is realized. As participants in this divine meal, we're not merely observers of a historic covenant but active partakers in the eternal kingdom established by Christ's sacrifice. Feeding on Christ and partaking in his suffering and victory, we find the strength to live lives that reflect God's glory, embodying his redemptive purpose in the world. This narrative doesn't just recount a transition in Israel's leadership; it calls us to live in the reality of

Christ's transformative presence, empowering us to reign with grace and truth.

> Afterward you will come to the hill of God where the Philistine garrison is; and it shall be as soon as you have come there to the city, that you will meet a group of prophets coming down from the high place with harp, tambourine, flute, and a lyre before them, and they will be prophesying. Then the Spirit of Yahweh will come upon you mightily, and you shall prophesy with them and be changed into another man. Now it will be when these signs come to you, do for yourself whatever your hand finds to do, for God is with you. And you shall go down before me to Gilgal; and behold, I will come down to you to offer burnt offerings and sacrifice peace offerings. You shall wait seven days until I come to you and make you know what you should do. (1 Sam. 10:5–8)

Positioned within the heart of a Philistine stronghold, a band of prophets presents a striking tableau of resistance, their arms bearing not the cold steel of swords or the sturdy wood of shields but the gentle curves of musical instruments. They are enveloped not in the armor of warriors but in the invisible, yet palpable, mantle of the Spirit's power. This assembly stands as a vivid counterpoint to the martial might and oppressive atmosphere that pervades their surroundings. They embody an alternative community, a beacon of light and hope within the larger, darker expanse of the dominant culture. Their presence and actions are a testament to the power of spiritual conviction over physical might, offering a profound commentary on the nature of true strength and resilience. Walter Brueggemann, in his seminal work, *The Prophetic Imagination*, articulates the essence of such a stance. He posits that the task of prophetic ministry is not merely to exist in opposition to the prevailing culture but to nurture, nourish, and evoke a consciousness that stands in stark contrast to the consciousness of the dominant culture. It's about awakening a different perception, one that sees beyond the immediate to the eternal, that values compassion over conquest, and that seeks justice and peace over dominance and discord.[11]

Their ecstatic prophesying, a dance of divine anticipation from an altered state of awareness, welcomes Saul into a realm of celebration that coexists and is juxtaposed to a world that amplifies the clamor of earthly conflict—a space where the future is sung, not seized by force. Saul slips into that otherworldly awareness, where metaphors expand the possibilities of his emotional breadth and depth inviting the kind of deep change that can lead to healing and wholeness. While the event symbolizes Saul's induction into a prophetic community under Samuel's guidance, it also signifies the invitation to a space where the gaps between where he is and where he longs to be can be afforded. It is a transition from the interior challenges he faces as "the son of Kish" to a new consciousness of being a "spiritual son" of Samuel the Seer. This was intended to be a support and strength to him as he moved into his future, not alone but with fatherly support that could come alongside him in his new role in a way that Kish could not. This realm of "seeing" was intended to be a way of seeing, a way of observing that would become a way of life. Imagine Saul, had he fully embraced Samuel's ways—his inspired speech, his visionary sight. Here stands Saul at a crossroads, not as a cautionary tale but as a beacon of what could be. He steps into the circle of prophets as a participant as well as an observer, invited into a realm where the divine speaks not just to but through him. Another Saul, generations later, will be triggered by his anger and his misplaced zeal and rage, that will drive him furiously on a great steed to race to Damascus to do "justice" to those who are disturbing his peace. Like the donkeys of Kish, those he seeks to find will evade his grasp. And while in pursuit, he will be brought, much like Saul of Gibeah, into an ecstatic state. However, this ecstatic state will blind him so that whatever the thought he could see, he will be prevented from seeing. Here in this moment, he will be confronted by a love that will not let him go. The Christ of the Damascus Road will blind this Saul in order to give him the sight he desperately needs. He will become one who is utterly constrained by the love that prevented him from allowing his emotional triggers to harm those whose very purpose was to embody the love of the One who is the Quintessential Mentor of Dreams of Destiny. In that, this Saul of Tarsus will become small in his own eyes (Paul) and will leave such a legacy behind for others to grow on that his name (Saul) will be mentioned for centuries and millennia in honorable and not tragic ways.

This isn't just about ancient history or theological debates; it's about the daily choices we make in how we live out our faith. It's about recognizing that the kingdom of God doesn't advance through coercion or political might but through acts of love, mercy, and justice that echo the life of Jesus. It's about asking ourselves whether our actions reflect the gospel's transformative power or the world's quest for control. Just as Saul was invited to step into a reality marked by prophetic speech and divine insight, so too are we called to embrace a path defined by openness to the Spirit's leading.

This ancient tableau offers us a mirror, reflecting the dissonance between the spiritual warfare of the kingdom and the battles we find ourselves entangled in today. In a time when the church's voice seems increasingly co-opted by the drumbeat of dominion, where the gospel is wielded like a weapon rather than extended as an invitation to grace, we stand at a crossroads. Have we, in our pursuit of influence, strayed from the path laid out by Jesus, whose message was always cruciform, always an embodiment of sacrificial love? The Spirit of prophecy, as revealed in Revelation 19:10, is not a call to arms but a testimony to Jesus. It's a reminder that the true power of the gospel lies not in the dominion it grants over others but in the transformation it brings to the human heart. Like Saul among the prophets, are we willing to let go of our conventional weapons and embrace a spiritual reality marked by change and possibility?

In the path that unfolds from Saul's encounter with the prophets, and Saul of Tarsus's encounter with the Quintessential Prophet and Seer, we catch a glimpse of what being faithful humans who reign in life by Christ Jesus might look like when rooted in the great prophetic tradition. It is a way of life that eschews the trappings of power for the power of the Spirit, that seeks not dominion but divine direction. It is here, in this space of potential and promise, that we find the segue into the reflection on how the church today might navigate the challenges of cultural dominion and the weaponization of the gospel. As we step forward from the hill of God, carrying the narrative of what Saul could have become, and what Saul of Tarsus did become, we are invited to reflect on how this potential can be realized in our own lives. How can we, like these figures at their best, enter into the ways of inspired speech and sight? How do we embody the prophetic spirit in a world that often values power over principle, domination over discipleship? This is not just a story of what was but a call to what could be. It's an invitation to walk in the footsteps of the prophets, to let our lives be instruments of God's peace, to let our actions speak of a Kingdom that is not of this world but is breaking into it with every act of love, every gesture of grace, every word of truth spoken in love. It is a call out of the shadows, an exodus out of the caves of our interior lives where we partner with dead things, and in coming into the light of the day of New Creation, we practice resurrection.

Notes

1. *The Matrix*, directed by Lana Wachowski and Lilly Wachowski (Burbank, CA: Warner Bros., 1999).
2. Telemachus sets out for Pylus under the guidance of the goddess Athene, who is disguised as Mentor, a friendly chief. (iii) Nestor, the aged king of

Pylus, receives them hospitably; and while he is banqueting his guests the supposed Mentor vanishes, and it is recognized that he was the guardian goddess of the family of Odysseus. Homer, *The Harvard Classics 22: The Odyssey of Homer*, ed. Charles W. Eliot, trans. S. H. Butcher and A. Lang (New York: P. F. Collier & Son, 1909), 4.

3. So with that word he sat him down; then in the midst up rose Mentor, the companion of noble Odysseus. He it was to whom Odysseus, as he departed in the fleet, had given the charge over all his house, that it should obey the old man, and that he should keep all things safe. Homer, *Harvard Classics 22*, 28.

4. Dean K. Thompson and D. Cameron Murchison, "Introduction," in *Mentoring: Biblical, Theological, and Practical Perspectives*, ed. Dean K. Thompson and D. Cameron Murchison (Grand Rapids, MI: Eerdmans, 2018), 1.

5. Thompson and Murchison, "Introduction," 2.

6. Susan Rattray, "Oak," ed. Mark Allan Powell, *HarperCollins Bible Dictionary*, rev. ed. (New York: HarperCollins, 2011), 712.

7. Rattray, "Oak," 712.

8. Leithart, *Son to Me*, 75.

9. Leithart, *Son to Me*, 75.

10. Leithart, *Son to Me*, 75.

11. Walter Brueggemann, *The Prophetic Imagination*, 2nd ed. (Minneapolis: Fortress Press, 2001), 3.